The Hertfordshire Batteries, Royal Field Artillery

An Illustrated History 1908–1920

Other titles by the author

Published by the Hertfordshire Local History Council:

Hertfordshire's Soldiers (1969)

Published by the Hertfordshire Yeomanry and Artillery Historical Trust:

Hertfordshire Yeomanry and Artillery Roll of Honour (1972)
Hertfordshire Yeomanry and Artillery Honours and Awards (1976)
Hertfordshire Yeomanry and Artillery Uniforms, Arms and Equipment (1980)

Published by Samson Books Ltd.:

'For Gallantry in the Performance of Military Duty' (1980)

Published by Hart Books, Welwyn:

'Hazardous Work' (1985)
A Guide to the History of the Bedfordshire and Hertfordshire Regiment (1987)
The Hertfordshire Yeomanry – An Illustrated History 1794–1920 (1994)

Published by Castlemead Publications:

The Hertfordshire Regiment – An Illustrated History (1988)

This book is dedicated to all those who have contributed to the achievements of the Hertfordshire Batteries, Royal Field Artillery in peace and war, but especially to those who fell in action in the Great War, 1914–1918.

"By what I've 'eard the others tell an' I in spots 'ave seen,
There's nothin' this side 'Eaven or 'Ell *Ubique* doesn't mean!"

Rudyard Kipling

Frontispiece   *A section of one of the Hertfordshire Batteries at exercise, c.1912. The two guns* (foreground), *with 6-horse teams, are each followed by their ammunition wagons, with 4-horse teams. Note the use of neck-collar draught harness, considered unsuitable for use by Territorial batteries because the collar had to be fitted to the horse and the same horses were not always available for training.*   (Regimental Collection)

The Hertfordshire Batteries, Royal Field Artillery

An Illustrated History
1908–1920

Lieutenant-Colonel J. D. SAINSBURY, T.D., F.S.A.

HART BOOKS, WELWYN

First Published 1996 by
Hart Books, Welwyn for the
Hertfordshire Yeomanry and
Artillery Historical Trust

British Library Cataloguing-in-Publication Data

A catalogue record for this book is available
from the British Library

ISBN 0–948527–04–8

Set in 11/12 Palatino

Printed and bound in Great Britain by

Stephen Austin and Sons Ltd., Hertford

Preface

This book may come as a surprise to those who read with any attention the preface to its immediate predecessor, *The Hertfordshire Yeomanry – An Illustrated History 1794–1920*, for there it was forecast that a history of the Hertfordshire Yeomanry and its successor units of the Royal Artillery would be completed in two volumes. That was, at the time, the intention of the Trustees of the Hertfordshire Yeomanry and Artillery Historical Trust but we have since agreed that the history of the Hertfordshire Batteries, and particularly the distinguished part they played in the campaign in Egypt and Palestine, should stand alone.

There has been a noticeable tendency over many years to minimise, or even to ignore, the original Gunner heritage of post-1920 artillery units in Hertfordshire. It was properly reflected, following amalgamation (*not* conversion), in the cumbersome title 86th (*East Anglian*) (Hertfordshire Yeomanry) Field Brigade, Royal Artillery but the 'East Anglian' designation was set aside during the Second World War and from 1947 onwards has not featured in unit titles. By 1967, in the face of further amalgamation and then reduction to a single battery – 201 (Hertfordshire and Bedfordshire Yeomanry) Battery, Royal Artillery (Volunteers) – based at Luton, this 'pure Gunner' ancestry had been diluted out of all recognition; indeed it had been lost. The move of part of 201 Battery to St. Albans offers the battery the opportunity of rebalancing their view of their heritage. I hope that this book will help them to do so. Comparisons of today's equipment and methods, successes and failures, should be made with those of the First World War, as well as those of the Second. The lesson, as always, will be that it is the human factors – courage, determination, resourcefulness, ingenuity – combined with the experience and skill acquired through training and in battle, that lead to real achievement.

The judgements I have made in this book are mine, unless attributed to others. The mistakes and omissions are mine too, though where the story looks 'thin' this is more likely to be due to absence of reliable source material than to intentional exclusion. The conventional 'Roll of Honour' and lists of honours and awards have been published in considerable detail by the Trust; those seeking details of other aspects of the batteries' history should refer to the Bibliography. The Trustees have again decided to go to press without maps and I would commend to those who wish to study the batteries' movements in more detail the maps in the *Official History* or the more modern publications by Bullock and Farndale, the latter of course concentrating on the deployment of the artillery during the campaign.

At risk of my repeated thanks becoming a mere convention, I must again refer to the many friends I have made while building the collection of documents, photographs and memories on which this history is based. Archivists, librarians and curators of all the institutions listed on the following page have gone far out of their way to help on so many occasions but I would like to single out Judithe Blacklaw of the Ministry of Defence Library and Brigadiers John Lewendon and Ken Timbers of the Royal Artillery Institution for particular thanks. I should also record the value that I attach to conversations held many years ago with Colonel Lord Oaksey (formerly Major Geoffrey Lawrence of 1st Hertfordshire Battery) and with Major Vivian Bailey, to whom I am also indebted for access to his diary. Professor Ian Beckett again gave advice on the background to the Auxiliary Forces set out in the first chapter; G.D. ('Bunny') Austin took on a role akin to that of research assistant in Peterborough; and Lilian Smith typed the whole of the manuscript with enthusiasm and skill. To all of these I am extremely grateful, but as always, it is not possible to mention by name everyone to whom thanks are due.

My wife has followed the historical trail with me for more than thirty years and has contributed much to the eventual publication of this series. 'The Regiment' owes her a lot, and for all her efforts on our behalf, and for her patience while 'the Regimental History' takes longer to finish than we all hoped, I again express my thanks.

J. D. Sainsbury
Welwyn, Hertfordshire
February 1996

Acknowledgements

The author and the trustees of the Hertfordshire Yeomanry and Artillery Historical Trust record their thanks to the following:

Army Museums Ogilby Trust

Bank of England Libraries

Cambridgeshire Library Service (Peterborough Library)

Commonwealth War Graves Commission

Corporation of London – Guildhall Library

Hertfordshire County Record Office

Hertfordshire Library Service
(especially Hertford and Watford Libraries)

Imperial War Museum – Department of Printed Books, Department of Photographs and Department of Records

Ministry of Defence – Military Secretary's Department, Army Medal Office and Central Library

National Army Museum – Department of Archives, Photographs, Film and Sound and Department of Fine and Decorative Art

Peterborough Museum and Art Gallery

Public Record Office

Royal Artillery Institution

Royal School of Artillery

University of London – Courtauld Institute of Art

They also express particular appreciation to:

The Director, National Army Museum for permission to reproduce Plate I from a copy of the chromolithograph in the Museum's collection.

Joan Wanklyn, for the inspiration and skill which she brought to the paintings at Plates II and III.

Henry Gray for once more providing drawings of badges and shoulder titles.

Joanne Farmer for the cover design.

Peter Davies and the late Fred Sellens for their help in photographing badges and in copying old photographs.

The Marquess of Salisbury for permission to reproduce the painting at Plate 1.

The Trustees of the Robert Kiln Charitable Trust.

Extracts from Crown Copyright publications and material in the Public Record Office are reproduced by permission of the Controller of Her Majesty's Stationery Office.

Contents

Coloured Plates

Plate 1   *Detail from a water-colour by Richard Livesay showing the signal gun, provided by the Horse Artillery Troop of the South Hertfordshire Yeomanry, at the Royal Review in Hatfield Park, June 1800. Volunteer artillery units raised to counter the threat of invasion by Revolutionary France were disbanded following the defeat of Napoleon, though a very small number of troops remained in service as part of the Yeomanry Cavalry, the last being disbanded in 1875.*
(The Marquess of Salisbury) (Photograph – Courtauld Institute of Art)

Chapter 1

Historical Background to the Territorial Artillery

The huge volunteer army raised between 1794 and 1808 to counter the threat of invasion from Revolutionary France contained a small artillery element, mainly for coastal defence. However, none of these corps survived the disbandments which followed the defeat of Napoleon and it was to units raised in 1859 and the early 1860s that most Territorial Force batteries looked for their history and traditions when they were formed in 1908.

The Artillery Volunteers, 1859–1908

By the spring of 1859, the threat of invasion from France had grown to such an extent that the government bowed to popular opinion and once more made provision for the Regular Army and the Militia to be supported by volunteers. A circular letter to Lords Lieutenant, dated 12th May 1859, sanctioned the formation of Volunteer Rifle and Artillery Corps under the authority of the Volunteer Consolidation Act, 1804,[1] the Act under which the Yeomanry Cavalry was raised. The 'Volunteer Force' was shortly expanded to include engineers, mounted rifles and   [1] light horse; medical, supply and transport and other supporting units were added later. The 1804 Act was recognised as unsatisfactory enabling legislation for the new force and was replaced by a new Volunteer Act in July 1863.[2] This brought up to date the administrative and disciplinary arrangements for volunteer forces other than the Yeomanry and, most importantly, enabled them to be maintained on a permanent footing in peace-time. Volunteers were now liable to be called out in case of "actual or apprehended invasion", whereas under the earlier Act they could not be called out until invasion was seen to be impending from the "appearance of the enemy in force upon the coast".

In his history of coast artillery, Maurice-Jones (see Bibliography) is scathing in his remarks about the Volunteers:

> "The Volunteer Artillery were never properly organised as either part of the field army or as coast artillery. They were mostly classified as 'position artillery', given such armament as was out of date and could be spared, and carried out their drill and training on these weapons firmly fixed to platforms let into the ground. What their role was to be in case of enemy invasion was never divulged. Some of the corps, whose headquarters were on the coast and near coast defence works, trained as coast artillery and were presumed to have their places on general mobilisation in the coast defences."

The Volunteer Artillery certainly did appear to have less than whole-hearted support from the Government. In part this may have been due to long-standing fears that their guns could be used in support of rebellion, but unwillingness to fund the necessary expenditure over many years was the over-riding reason for their out-dated armament and techniques. (It must, in fairness, be observed that the Regular component of the coast defences was hardly equipped with the most up-to-date weapons, either.) Furthermore, there was a widespread feeling, unjustified as it turned out, that volunteers could never fully master the intricacies of mobile artillery and should only be let loose on fixed equipments.

The role of the Yeomanry Cavalry and the Volunteer Infantry in the event of invasion was at least as doubtful as that of the Volunteer Artillery but Maurice-Jones ignores the original purpose of the Artillery Volunteer Corps, as laid down in a War Office Circular dated 25th May 1859 and quoted by Berry (see Bibliography):

> "As regards Artillery Volunteers, their primary object will be to aid, in the most efficient manner, in the manning of the batteries erected for the protection of our coast towns, so that the Royal Artillery and Militia may be, to as great extent as possible, disposable for other services."

A further circular, dated 13th July 1859, directed the attention of Lords Lieutenant of maritime counties to the desirability of forming Artillery, rather than Rifle, Volunteer Corps and, pointed out that:

> "In case of war the vast number of guns mounted in our coast defences will require a large Artillery force to work them, and the Volunteers can in no way be so useful to the public service as when formed in Artillery Corps to man the batteries, and thus release a proportionate force of Royal Artillery for service in the field."

Accordingly, preference would be given to the formation of Artillery Corps wherever coast batteries were already available for practice. They could also usefully be formed "at places on the sea coast at which batteries do not now exist but where the Military Authorities may deem it advisable to place guns hereafter", provided that the members of the corps, aided as necessary by the local population, "would take upon themselves the erection of earthworks". The three functions of the Volunteer Artillery thus comprised the manning of existing fixed coast defence armament, the provision of mobile batteries of suitable calibre and range for the occupation of emergency coastal gun positions which had been previously prepared and, later, the provision of artillery support for troops defending vulnerable points on the coast from attack from flanks or rear by an enemy force that had landed elsewhere on the coast. Artillery Volunteer Corps formed in inland counties could readily train for the last two of these functions.

In 1889, the various Volunteer Artillery Corps were taken under command of the 'garrison divisions', and thus formally incorporated in the coast defence order of battle,[3] and in 1902 they were all redesignated as Royal Garrison Artillery (Volunteers).[4] Changes in command or in title did little to improve their armament, but the restriction of the Volunteers to fixed or

Plate 2 *Volunteer artillerymen at drill with a 40-pdr. R.M.L. gun, late 1890s. Although the idea that the Volunteer Artillery should be restricted to guns in fixed emplacements had by now been abandoned, they were equipped with clumsy and outdated weapons until well after the turn of the century.* (from 'Navy and Army Illustrated')

semi-mobile equipments had by now to a great extent been set aside. A bewildering variety of guns were in use during the 1890s and early 1900s, many of them muzzle-loading patterns introduced more than thirty years earlier. Some corps were armed with 9-pdr. or 13-pdr. fully-mobile field guns but the majority of those whose role was outside the permanent fixed emplacements had either 16-pdr. or 40-pdr. guns. If photographs are to be believed, these required heavier draught horses and would have moved correspondingly slowly. That the Volunteer Artillery, in common with the Yeomanry and the Volunteer Infantry, was overdue for reform by the turn of the century is hardly in doubt. Their predicament is nicely illustrated by a commentary on the 4th West Riding of Yorkshire R.G.A.(V.) which appeared in *The Navy and Army Illustrated* of 28th February 1903:

> "It is a great pity that the Government have not seen their way to supply the various Volunteer Artillery Corps . . . with more modern guns than those with which they are at present equipped . . . The 4th West Riding . . . is a corps in which both officers and men take a great interest in their work, and should certainly receive some encouragement from the Government in the matter of armament. The guns with which the brigade is now equipped consist of old 16-pounder muzzle-loaders, practically worn out and still fired with black powder, which were discarded by the Army as obsolete some twenty years ago.
>
> As far back as 1900 Lord Lansdowne declared in the House of Commons his intention of supplying the Volunteer Artillery with 4.7-in. and 15-pounder breech-loading guns, but here the matter seems to have ended, for no further steps in the right direction have as yet been taken. Surely it cannot be that the Secretary of State for War and the War Office experts who are his advisers are desirous of damping the patriotic enthusiasm of the thousands of officers and men who have been patiently waiting for the last three years for the promise of more modern armament to be redeemed!"

'Redemption' was not in fact to come until 1908, when despite all the difficulties, there were, in addition to the Honourable Artillery Company, 65 units of Royal Garrison Artillery (Volunteers), by no means all of them recruited on or near the coast.

The Territorial Force, 1908–1914

Among the many reforms carried out in the light of the British Army's experience in the South African War, 1899–1902, was a complete reorganisation of the land defences of the United Kingdom, which were to be placed entirely in the hands of part-time, volunteer soldiers. [3]

Plate 3 *The 'Imperial Service' badge introduced by Army Order 3 of 1910 for wear by members of the Territorial Force who had volunteered to serve outside the British Isles on mobilisation.* (Regimental Collection)

Under the direction of the Secretary of State for War, R.B. Haldane (later Viscount Haldane of Cloan), plans were made in 1906 for a new 'Territorial Force' to be formed from the existing Imperial Yeomanry and Volunteer Force. It was fundamental to Haldane's scheme that the Territorial Force would be organised in divisions, with a proper balance of arms and services. Ideally, over 300,000 volunteers would form fourteen divisions, each based in a different part of the country (hence the description 'Territorial'), with extra troops, mainly artillery and engineers, for fixed coast defences. The implications of these far-reaching ideas, which depended to a great extent on large-scale, and willing, transfers from the Imperial Yeomanry and the Volunteer Force, were debated for some time. A proposal for extensive use of the new volunteers abroad on mobilisation was substantially modified. Otherwise, the plans for complete reorganisation and reform were generally adopted, though not without opposition, and new enabling legislation was passed, as the Territorial and Reserve Forces Act, 1907,[5] to come into effect on 1st April 1908.

The Territorial and Reserve Forces Act, 1907 did not repeal the Volunteer Act, 1863, which was used again during the First World War (see below). It empowered the Crown "to raise and maintain a force, to be called the Territorial Force, consisting of such men as may from time to time be provided by Parliament". On embodiment, which could only take place after call-out of the First Class of the Army Reserve, men of the Territorial Force could be required to serve in any part of the United Kingdom but they could not be ordered abroad. However, in reflection of Haldane's idea that the Territorial Force should be available for the reinforcement of an expeditionary force, the Crown could accept offers of units or individual officers and men to serve outside the United Kingdom (the so-called 'Imperial Service' obligation) and to be called out for deployment in the United Kingdom before the embodiment of the Territorial Force as a whole. The administration, including recruiting and clothing, of the Territorial Force was placed in the hands of 'County Associations' – statutory bodies consisting of serving and retired officers and civilians, with a small number of full-time officials.

A Special Army Order dated 18th March 1908 gave full details of the organisation and peace establishments of the Territorial Force;[6] war establishments were published a year later.[7] There was a massive increase in the number of artillery units compared with the Volunteer Force. Each of the fourteen infantry divisions included three 3-battery brigades armed with 15-pdr. field guns and one 2-battery brigade armed with 5-in. howitzers. A heavy battery, Royal Garrison Artillery of four 4.7-in. guns was also assigned to each division. The fourteen mounted brigades all incorporated a battery of Royal Horse Artillery (four 15-pdr. Q.F. guns) and there were 81 Royal Garrison Artillery companies to man the coast defences. Whereas the mounted troops and the infantry of the Territorial Force were raised by straightforward conversion of existing regiments of the Imperial Yeomanry and infantry battalions of the Volunteer Force, the overwhelming majority of the 182 horse, field, howitzer and heavy batteries required in the Territorial Force, and their associated ammunition columns, were raised from scratch. Although most of them were sponsored by existing units of the Royal Garrison Artillery (Volunteers), the changes in establishment, involving considerable recruiting, and in the tactics and training associated with their new role as 'divisional artillery', were such as to render the new units unrecognisable from the old. At least 135 of

[4]

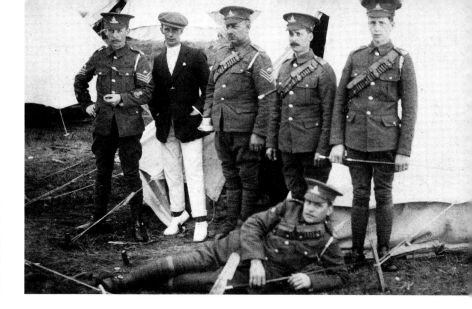

Plate 4 *A smart group of non-commissioned officers and men of 1st Herts Battery about to 'walk out' from camp, c.1910. The prospect of a fortnight's annual training by the sea was a significant factor in attracting recruits to Territorial batteries.* (Regimental Collection)

the new batteries traced their heritage from the Royal Garrison Artillery (Volunteers); in counties without R.G.A. units it was normally infantry battalions of the Volunteer Force that provided the cadres for new batteries. The Royal Garrison Artillery companies in the coast defences were formed by conversion, in some cases with reorganisation, of earlier coast artillery units. The peace and war establishments of Territorial field batteries differed little and, importantly, there was no provision for the 4-gun battery to expand to the 6-gun war establishment of its Regular counterpart. (The tactics, organisation and deployment of the field batteries are explained in Chapter 2.)

Khaki service dress was adopted as standard throughout the Territorial Force. The wearing of full dress was strictly controlled and in general confined to officers, but units were permitted to provide other ranks with a 'walking-out' uniform, which was worn on certain parades and when off duty. A common pattern of shoulder title for other ranks was prescribed by *Territorial Force Regulations*. It consisted of the county or other title surmounted by the letters T. – R.F.A. or T. – R.G.A. The cap badge for all ranks was the standard Royal Artillery pattern with the word '*Ubique*' on the upper scroll replaced by a sprig of laurel leaves. (Territorial units were not at this stage allowed to carry battle honours that they had not themselves earned.)

The First World War

The Territorial Force was embodied and mobilised on the outbreak of war in August 1914 at a strength of about 250,000, of which about 35,000 were Gunners. It was at once clear that the best use of Territorial units could only be made if they served abroad, either with the British Expeditionary Force in France or in relief of Regular troops in distant garrisons. Efforts were accordingly made to encourage whole units to volunteer for Imperial Service, in general with success. The raising of additional units of the Territorial Force to take the place within the United Kingdom defences of units that had volunteered for service abroad, and to provide a training organisation, was first authorised in August 1914.[8] The exact role of these units, their designations and the arrangements for their administration evolved, not without some confusion, over the next two-and-a-half years.

Plate 5 *The gun cap badge of the Royal Field Artillery as worn by units of the Territorial Force. On the upper scroll the word 'Ubique' has been replaced by a sprig of laurel leaves under regulations which prevented units of the Auxiliary Forces from carrying honours awarded to their Regular counterparts.*
(Regimental Collection) [5]

Plate 6 *A 1st Line Territorial brigade of the Royal Field Artillery – three batteries, each of four 15-pdr. B.L.C. guns – at exercise in 1915. The ammunition wagons that accompanied each gun are not shown.* (From 'Kitchener's Army . . .')

Each brigade (field or howitzer) or battery (horse or heavy) that proceeded abroad was to be backed by two equivalent units at home, though shortages of guns and instruments prevented these units from being recruited at once to full establishment. 'Reserve' brigades/batteries were formed in September 1914 "to take the place . . . of the Imperial Service unit if, and when, the latter is ordered abroad" and "to act as a feeder to replace wastage in the Imperial Service unit".[9] Reserve units were initially manned by those who had not volunteered to serve abroad or were not of the required medical standard, but their composition changed as the war progressed. The aged and infirm were weeded out and a substantial proportion, at least until mid-1916, were men fit for general service and awaiting posting abroad. In November 1914, Reserve units were redesignated '1st Reserve' in consequence of the raising of '2nd Reserve' units (see below).[10] From the end of January 1915, their second-line status was shown by 2/ in front of the designation of the original unit, which itself took 1/ in front of its title.[11] Curiously, it was not until the end of February 1915 that the descriptions '1st Line', '2nd Line' and '3rd Line', which had been in use for some time, were officially introduced to replace 'Imperial Service', '1st Reserve' and '2nd Reserve'.[12]

In November 1914, the formation of 2nd Reserve units at the depot or peace-time head-quarters of original Territorial units was authorised.[13] The authority was extensively amended at the end of December[14] to clarify the establishment of 2nd Reserve units, which differed according to whether the Imperial Service unit had "proceeded abroad to join the Expeditionary Force" or had embarked "for service elsewhere than with the Expeditionary Force". The role of the 2nd Reserve (later 3rd Line) unit was to act as a training and draft-pro-
[6] ducing depot for both the 1st and 2nd Line units and the higher or lower establishment evi-

dently reflected the likelihood of casualties and the requirement for replacement drafts. These units were frequently referred to as '3rd Line Depots', which led to confusion with the unit depots already constituted on mobilisation.[15] In present-day terminology 'training brigade/battery' would be the most apt description of the 3rd Line artillery unit.

Shortages of guns and other equipment and horses, and the need to make the best possible use of the few well qualified instructors, led to the formation during May and June 1915 of five Territorial Force Artillery Training Schools – four for training personnel for units armed with the 15-pdr. gun and one for those going to units armed with the 5-in. howitzer or the 4.7-in. heavy gun.[16] Each 3rd Line unit was affiliated to one of the schools, which became responsible for training all ranks to the standard required for drafting to a 1st or 2nd Line unit within three months.[17] The schools thus needed to be capable of handling as many as 1,500 trainees at a time. In November 1915, instructions were issued for 3rd Line artillery units to concentrate at the training school to which they were affiliated and the units themselves ceased to exist.[18] The schools were subject to some reorganisation between formation and August 1916, when the eight schools then existing were designated Nos. 1 to 8 Reserve Brigades, Royal Field Artillery, Territorial Force.[19]

In April 1915, it was decided that personnel serving with 2nd Line Territorial units who were available only for Home Service were to be removed from those units and formed into 'Provisional Units for Home Defence'.[20] It was expected that the Provisional units, which would not be liable to find reinforcement drafts for overseas, would become efficient more rapidly than 2nd Line Territorial units and would thus be able to take an effective part in the defence of the British Isles against enemy attack sooner. The standing and role of Provisional units was confirmed in July 1915, when instructions were given that "whenever possible and   [7] advantageous, the Provisional units of Home Service T.F. personnel . . . should, as far as practicable, be organised into Provisional Brigades of all arms", [21] and War Establishments for Provisional Brigades were issued. [22] A brigade would be composed of four infantry battalions, a Yeomanry squadron, a cyclist company, a battery of Royal Field Artillery, a field company, Royal Engineers and medical and supply and transport units. Only ten Provisional Brigades were formed, but each brigade included a Provisional Battery, R.F.A. which took its designation from its brigade, 1 Provisional Battery serving with 1 Provisional Brigade, etc. According to the instructions, the Provisional Brigades would "form a first line for protection against raids, behind which the 2nd Line Territorial divisions will complete their organisation and training". By the end of 1915, ten brigades had been formed, each including its own Provisional battery. There were a further nineteen battalions, but only one field battery, that were 'unbrigaded'.

When instructions for the reconstitution of the force were issued in December 1916, [23] only the ten brigades were retained. Until now, all Provisional units had been composed of attached personnel, who remained on the supernumerary posted strength of their 2nd Line Territorial units. Reconstitution, which took effect on 1st January 1917, involved the creation of new Territorial units to take the place of the Provisional units, and personnel being posted to the new units. The former 1–10 Provisional Batteries were reconstituted as numbered batteries and were allocated the block 1203–1212 in a series set aside for war-formed batteries. Each battery adopted a subsidiary designation indicating the divisional area from which its personnel were drawn, e.g. 1203 (Lowland) Battery, R.F.A. Three of these batteries had already joined Home Service divisions with their brigades in November 1916 and four more became part of 67th Divisional Artillery late in 1917. The other three batteries remained independent of divisional command.

The obviously cumbersome titles of the brigades that formed the divisional artillery of both 1st and 2nd Line Territorial divisions were abandoned in May 1916 in favour of a numbered series following on from Regular and New Army brigades. Officially, brigades were styled in Roman numerals, beginning with CCX (210), allocated to 1st/1st East Lancashire Brigade of 42nd Division, and ending with CCCXLVIII (348), which fell to 2nd/4th East Anglian Brigade of 69th Division. [24] (Not all the numbers in the series were taken up.) The new Roman series was hardly less cumbersome than the designations it replaced and confusion was common. Accordingly, the Roman numerals were frequently, but unofficially, discarded in favour of Arabic. (The Roman designations are ignored entirely in the *Official Histories* but set out in full in *Order of Battle of Divisions*.) Within each brigade, the constituent batteries lost their local titles and were lettered 'A', 'B' or 'C' according to their former seniority. Later reorganisations, notably when Territorial batteries were increased from four guns to six, gave rise to changes in brigade designations, which took place within the original Roman series.

Substantial changes in the administration of the Territorial artillery were introduced in November 1916. There was by now increasing emphasis on the brigade as a unit and transfers between the batteries of a brigade were becoming commonplace. Yet, frequently, batteries within a brigade were recruited in different counties and were thus administered by different Territorial Associations. With a view to removing the "complications and risk of error" occasioned by this system, instructions were issued reallocating Territorial artillery units to Associations "on the basis of complete brigades". [25] At almost the same time, instructions were also given for the renumbering, with effect from 1st January 1917 (later amended to 15th February 1917), of other ranks from a series which allotted blocks of numbers to each County Association, and for the centralisation of soldiers' documents and pay accounts at Woolwich (R.H. and R.F.A) and Dover (R.G.A.). [26] The Royal Artillery components of existing Territorial Force depots were concentrated in February 1917 at the Royal Horse Artillery Depot at Woolwich and at Royal Field Artillery and Royal Garrison Artillery Depots in each command. [27]

Following disembodiment in 1919, all those units which had been formed during the war were disbanded. Those in being before the war were dispersed at their home stations – a formality sometimes carried out by half a dozen men with a trunkful of records – and for a time, while decisions were made on their future, they existed only on paper.

Territorial Gunner units served in all major theatres during 'The Great War, 1914–18', as it was to become officially known. The custom in the Royal Regiment of Artillery is that no

Plate 7 *An 18-pdr. gun with 6-horse team from 1st/1st Hertfordshire Battery taking part in a turn-out and driving competition in Egypt, probably 1916. By this time all 1st Line Territorial Divisions were serving abroad and their artillery units had become considerably 'diluted' by officers and soldiers who had joined after the declaration of war.* (Regimental Collection)

individual battle honours are granted to units. As a mark of the achievements of the whole of the Territorial Force during the war, however, units of all arms were granted the privilege of bearing the honours gained by their Regular counterparts on their colours and appointments.[28] Territorial Gunners accordingly adopted the Regular pattern of cap badge and have since been recognised as contributing fully to the accumulating total of actions and achievements that constitute '*Ubique*'.

The Volunteer Force, 1916–1918

The government was at first reluctant to take up offers of volunteer service in the country's immediate defence during the First World War, fearing that voluntary recruitment into the Regular Army, the New Armies and the Territorial Force would suffer. In November 1914, however, a considerable measure of control was brought over the many local volunteer units that had been formed by enforcing affiliation to the Central Association of Volunteer Training Corps. Units of the Volunteer Training Corps were exclusively infantry, with a small number of motor car owners forming the associated National Motor Volunteers, but there is some evidence that members of infantry battalions raised in north-east England were trained to assist in the manning of fixed coast artillery defences. Early in 1916, government policy of keeping the volunteers at arm's length was reversed in favour of recognising them as part of the Armed Forces of the Crown, and the dormant Volunteer Acts, 1863–1900 were resuscitated in April to enable the Crown to accept offers of service in a new 'Volunteer Force'. *Regulations for the Volunteer Force* were issued, county Territorial Force Associations responded to an invitation to take over the administration of the Volunteer Force, and officers received commissions. Supplementary legislation was introduced later in the year [29]to enable those members of Volunteer units who were able, and wished, to do so to perform duties in addition to those required under the 1863 Act. The Volunteers were thus able to undertake a range of useful tasks, such as the guarding of prisoners of war or vulnerable points, and make a contribution to manpower savings.

The first artillery corps was officially recognised – as the East Yorkshire Volunteer Garrison Artillery – in January 1917,[30] and a further seven corps were later accepted.[31] The eight corps provided between them eleven companies. The requirement for Volunteer anti-aircraft troops was met by the use of specially trained personnel from the infantry battalions, rather than by raising additional corps of artillery. In July 1918, the constitution of the Volunteer Force was changed, and infantry battalions were allowed to adopt designations as Volunteer battalions of their county regiments and wear the appropriate badges. At the same time, artillery units were designated as, e.g., East Yorkshire Royal Garrison Artillery (Volunteers)[32] and badged accordingly. Recruiting and compulsory training for the Volunteer Force ceased in December 1918, when the units stood down, but formal disbandment did not start until September of the following year, to be completed in March 1920.[33]

Plate 8 *A draft about to leave Peterborough, probably late 1914–early 1915. The responsibility for training reinforcements for 1st Line Territorial units lay with the '3rd Line Depots' of each brigade until it was assumed by the Territorial Force Artillery Training Schools in November 1915.* (Regimental Collection)

The Territorial Force re-formed, 1920

Recruiting for the post-war Territorial Force opened in February 1920, after nearly a year of discussion – within the War Office, between the War Office and County Associations, and in Parliament. Much of the debate concerned the revised terms of service that the experience of the past ten years had shown would be necessary, but the order of battle, too, needed substantial change.

At his first meeting with County Associations on 1st April 1919, the Secretary of State for War, Winston Churchill, made clear that the new Territorial Force would be liable for service overseas, though not until any future emergency had become "so serious that a general Military Service Act has been assented to by Parliament for the whole of the rest of the country". Referring to the question of organisation, the Secretary of State said that it was proposed and recommended "that the Territorial Force shall be reconstituted, and that it shall be organised, as described in Paragraph 1 of *Territorial Force Regulations*, into fourteen divisions, fourteen mounted brigades, army troops, garrison and line of communication units". The plan envisaged re-creating pre-war 1st Line Territorial Force units "subject, of course, to such modifications in their character as the progress of modern weapons may render necessary".[34] Discussion with representatives of the Council of Territorial Associations took place at intervals until another general meeting, again chaired by the Secretary of State, was held on 1st May. Here, the order of battle was dealt with at greater length and it became apparent in the answers to questions about the future of coast defence units and the Yeomanry that, although the government's declared intention was to reconstitute the Territorial Force of 1914, they completely reserved their position on the question of whether units, particularly of the Yeomanry, would retain their historic role or be forced, through the exigencies of modern war, to undergo drastic change.[35] In general, however, the artillery were not threatened and could be certain of a key role, both in divisions, in army troops and in coast defence.

The arguments rumbled on until, faced with the necessity of making an announcement to Parliament in the forthcoming debate on the Army Estimates, Churchill, together with the Army Council and a number of other senior officers from the War Office, met representatives of County Associations for the last time on 30th January 1920. He announced that the reconstituted force would have its title changed to 'Territorial Army', and confirmed the obligation to serve abroad on mobilisation, though subject to the passing of a confirmatory Act of Parliament. Recruiting would begin during February. The previous commitment to fourteen mounted brigades was abandoned and it was made clear that, out of the 55 existing regiments of Yeomanry, less than twenty would retain their traditional mounted role. (As things turned out, the fourteen regiments highest in the order of precedence remained mounted and two regiments retained their horses and were shown in the *Army List* as 'Scouts'.) The remainder would re-role as artillery, armoured car or signals units.[36]

The artillery probably suffered less than any other arm in the transformation from Territorial Force to Territorial Army, which took more than two years to complete. Their role was assured – and, indeed, would soon be expanded to include air defence; there were huge [10] stocks of up-to-date weapons and equipment; and officers and men with formidable war experience could confidently be expected to form the nucleus of the new units, both as Territorials and as members of the permanent staff. From every point of view it looked as if the Territorial artillery was fit to face the future.

NOTES:
1. 44 Geo. III c.54 (see Appendix 1)
2. 26 & 27 Vict, c.65 (see Appendix 1)
3. Army Orders 443 and 482/1889
4. Army Order 27/1902
5. 7 Edw. VII c.9 (see Appendix 1)
6. Army Order 70/1908
7. Army Order 17/1909 (See Appendix 2)
8. A.C.I. 310/Aug. 1914
9. Army Order 399/1914;
   A.C.I. 198/Oct.1914
10. A.C.I. 271/Nov. 1914
11. A.C.I. 258/Jan. 1915
12. A.C.I. 229/Feb. 1915
13. A.C.I. 271/Nov. 1914
14. A.C.I. 266/Dec. 1914
15. Army Order 226/1914
16. A.C.I. 212/May 1915;
    A.C.I.s 122 and 213/June 1915;
    A.C.I. 1/July 1915
17. A.C.I. 81/Oct. 1915
18. A.C.I. 129/Nov.1915
19. A.C.I. 1588/1916
20. A.C.I. 220/Apr. 1915
21. A C.I. 31/July 1915
22. Army Order 314/1915
23. A.C.I. 2364/1916
24. W.O.L. 9/General/6051(T.F.1) of 7th June 1916
25. A.C.I. 2185/1916
26. A.C.I.s 2198 and 2438/1916 and 172/1917
27. A.C.I. 347/1917
28. Army Order 298/1917
29. 6 & 7 Geo.V c.62 (see Appendix 1)
30. Army Order 23/1917
31. Army Orders 305 and 358/1917;
    Army Order 110/1918 (see also *The Volunteer Force List*)
32. Army Order 208/1918
33. Army Order 455/1920
34. *Report of Proceedings at a Conference between the Secretary of State for War and Representatives of the Territorial Force Associations – 1st April 1919*
35. *Report of Proceedings . . . 1st May 1919*
36. *Report of Proceedings . . . 30th January 1920*

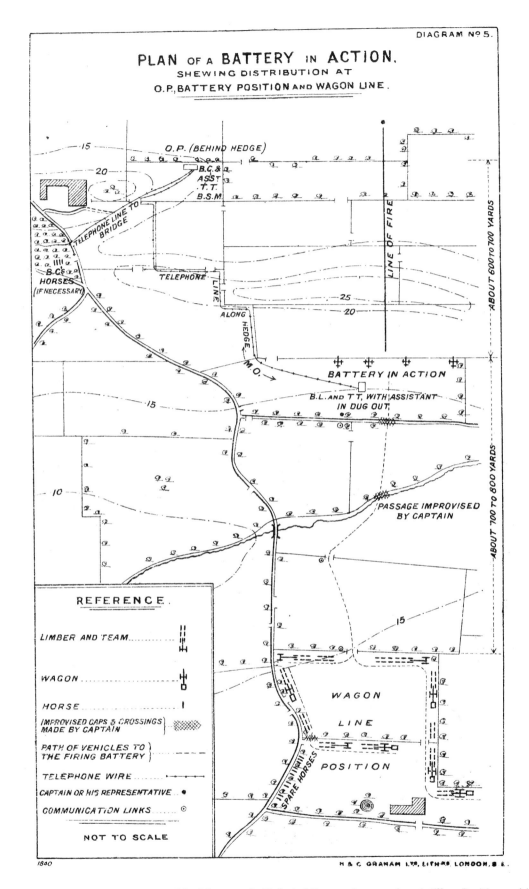

Plate 9 *Diagram from the training pamphlet 'Notes on the Technical Reconnaissance of an Artillery Position . . .' (April 1917) showing a 4-gun battery in action. The symbol 'TT' at the O.P. and on the gun position represents a signaller-telephonist, while 'BL' on the gun position indicates the battery leader, one of the section commanders, who was responsible for bringing the guns on to the position and deploying them in accordance with the intentions of the reconnaissance officer ('RO'), whose station during deployment was at the director.*

[12]   (Royal Artillery Institution)

Chapter 2

The Development of Field Artillery Tactics, Organisation and Equipment, 1900–1920

Experience in the South African War (1899–1902) forced the Royal Regiment of Artillery, no less than other branches of the Army, to revise rapidly, and in the field, tactics which had held good for the greater part of the nineteenth century. In the face of aimed fire at long range from high velocity rifles and machine-guns, batteries were frequently obliged to deploy in covered positions, e.g., behind reverse slopes. This, in turn, forced a shift away from direct fire (i.e., targets upon which guns are directly sighted optically) to increasingly widespread use of indirect fire (i.e., the engagement of targets by an observer who can see the target with guns which are not directly optically sighted). These changes in tactics were facilitated, and indeed to an extent led, by improvements in the design of field guns, notably the introduction in France, in 1897, of the now famous 75-mm. gun, which set new standards of stability in action and rate of fire that other nations sought quickly to copy. In Britain, the specifications for a new 'family' of guns were agreed in the early 1900s and the guns themselves – the 13-pdr. and 18-pdr. field guns and the 4.5-in. howitzer – were in service with Regular units by the outbreak of war in 1914.

These changes in tactics and equipment should have brought with them greater changes in application of fire and in command and control of artillery in battle than in fact they did. The requirement now was for co-ordinated fire support for the cavalry and infantry in all phases of the battle but little was done to change doctrine which had been in force for over one hundred years and which, for practical purposes, restricted artillery to the opening stages of a battle. Notably, the artillery retained an independent command structure which did not make for ready integration into a divisional or higher commander's battle plan; and no attempt was made to start the close affiliation at lower tactical levels between cavalry and infantry commanders and their supporting artillery officers that proved eventually to be so necessary.

Within the 'Field Branch' (i.e., all units whose primary role is to engage ground targets, regardless of the range or calibre of their guns), this book is concerned only with what are now termed 'close support' units. The key functions within a close support battery have not varied since the early years of the century. They are:

1. Target acquisition, normally carried out by forward observers – the Battery Commander's and observation post ('O.P.') parties – linked to the guns by one or more signalling systems.

2. Reconnaissance, selection and occupation of gun positions and control of the guns in action, carried out by the 'R' (=Reconnaissance) and 'C.P.' (= Command Post) groups, traditionally known as the 'Battery Staff'.

3. The guns themselves, together with their ready-use ammunition.

4. Immediate resupply of ammunition, and, later, fuel ('A' Echelon).

5. Administration and logistics ('B' Echelon).

CARRIAGE, FIELD, B.L.C. 15 PR, MARK I.

INCHES

CARRIAGE, FIELD, B.L.C. 15 PR MARK I.

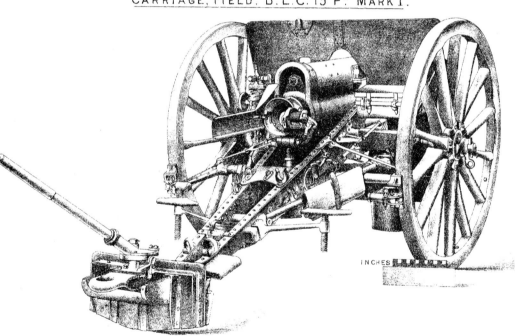

INCHES

Plate 10 *Ordnance B.L. Converted 15-pdr. Gun Mk.I on Carriage Mk.I. The gun is readily recognisable by the 'shroud' over the recoil system and its 14-spoke wheels. Its maximum range was 5,750 yards.*
(Royal Artillery Institution)

During the First World War, the emphasis moved up from the battery to higher levels, and techniques had to be evolved for grouping large numbers of guns of various calibres in support of divisions and higher formations. This placed extra demands on signal communications and survey, especially at the level immediately above the battery, i.e., the lieutenant-colonel's command or 'brigade', which were met by increases from time to time in the role, and hence the establishment, of brigade headquarters. Whatever changes took place to establish and improve higher levels of command, however, the battery remained the key unit. Within the Royal Regiment of Artillery it is the lowest level of command capable of [14] operating independently from all tactical and administrative points of view and, indeed,

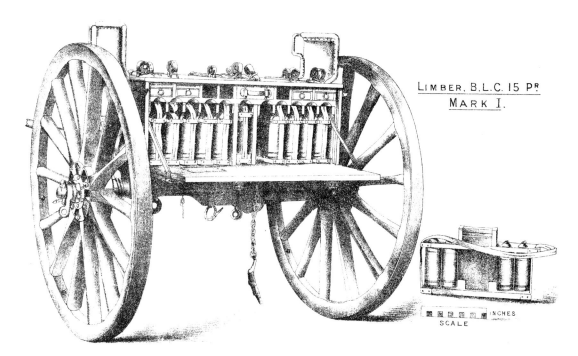

LIMBER, B.L.C. 15 PR
MARK I.

INCHES
SCALE

Plate 11 *The 15-pdr.*
limber and wagon.
Top – The limber,
used with gun and
wagon, showing the
storage for 40 rounds
of ammunition.
Bottom – The
ammunition wagon,
which carried 50
rounds.
(Royal Artillery
Institution)

WAGON, AMMUNITION AND LIMBER, B.L.C. 15 PR. MARK I.

SCALE
INCHES

while in the cavalry and infantry a lieutenant-colonel's command (regiment or battalion) is sub-divided into squadrons or companies commanded by majors, in the Royal Regiment majors' commands (batteries) are grouped into regiments (formerly brigades) commanded by lieutenant-colonels. Batteries are numbered and are the focal point for all aspects of morale, including history and tradition.

Throughout the period from 1908 to the beginning of the First World War, the tactics, and hence the training, of Territorial field artillery were similar to those of their Regular counterparts, but there were differences in establishment that were sometimes significant, and the Territorials' peacetime equipment scales were not only well below Regular scales but the [15]

Plate 12 *15-pdr. B.L.C. guns of a 2nd Line Territorial Division parked at Huntingdon, probably 1915. This photograph affords a good view of the 15-pdr. ammunition wagon and its limber* (foreground).
(Regimental Collection)

equipment itself was usually outdated, if not actually obsolete. While there were considerable technical advances during the First World War, both in the application of artillery fire and in signal communications above battery level, the equipment, organisation and deployment of field batteries, including Territorial batteries, changed very little until mechanisation, which did not begin until well after the war was over.

On formation in 1908, Territorial batteries of the Royal Field Artillery were issued with the 15-pdr. 'Breach-loading, Converted' (B.L.C.) gun or the 5-in. howitzer. The 15-pdr., which first came into service in 1900, had been designed without any recoil-dampening mechanism. 'Conversion', carried out in 1907, consisted principally of rebuilding the carriage to accommodate a buffer-recuperator, which must have contributed significantly to stability in action, and hence rate of fire (see above). The maximum ranges of the gun and howitzer were 5,750 yards and 6,500 yards, respectively, the latter only achievable with a reduced-weight (40-pound) shell.

After mobilisation, 1st Line Territorial batteries were re-equipped with the 18-pdr. field gun and the 4.5-in. howitzer before proceeding abroad. The 18-pdr. fired a heavier shell than the 15-pdr. B.L.C. but the early marks of pole-trail carriage limited the elevation of the barrel, and its maximum range, at 6,525 yards, was little better than that of its predecessor. In contrast, the 4.5-in. howitzer fired a rather lighter shell than the 5-in. but outranged it and the new 18-pdr. by some eight hundred yards at its maximum range of 7,300 yards. Shortages of guns were such, in 1914 and 1915, that 2nd and 3rd Line batteries were often forced to rely on mock-up wooden guns mounted on handcarts for their early training, and later on obsolete British equipments and a very limited supply of equally antique French 90-mm. field guns. The situation improved as 15-pdr. B.L.C.s and 5-in. howitzers were released from 1st Line to 2nd Line units, but it was not until the beginning of 1916 that the supply position had improved to the extent that 18-pdrs. and 4.5-in. howitzers could be issued to units at home.

Modifications were made to both the 18-pdr. and the 4.5-in. howitzer as the war progressed but none significantly affected the appearance of the guns, or, more importantly, their range. It was only in the last few weeks of the war in France that a considerably redesigned 18-pdr. made its appearance. The Mk. IV barrel on Mk. III box-trail carriage was able to attain a range of 9,300 yards through much greater elevation than had been possible with the pole trail. This gun did not enter service in the Egypt–Palestine theatre and its significance was much more as a 'between-the-wars' weapon and as the forerunner of the standard British field gun of the Second World War, the 25-pdr.

Throughout the First World War, a battery was established to provide only one observation post, manned by the battery commander, who had a small staff – technical assistant, range-taker and signallers. Additional forward observation teams were drawn from the gun position as the operational situation dictated. Communication between the observation post and the
[16] gun position was ideally by telephone and the establishment of signallers provided for teams

Plate 13 *Ordnance Q.F. 18-pdr. Gun Mk.II on Carriage Mk.II. Its maximum range was restricted to 6,525 yards by the pole trail.* (Royal Artillery Institution)

of operators and line maintenance parties. Equipment for flag, lamp and heliograph signalling was held and these methods were used as appropriate instead of, or as back up to, line.

On deployment, the general area of the gun position was selected by the battery commander, who would indicate it, together with the line of fire, to the gun position officer, either visually or by map reference, and move on to his observation post position. The gun position officer then marked the position of the 'pivot' gun, the alignment of the line of guns and the direction of the line of fire. The 'battery leader' (a subaltern officer) brought the guns on to the position to come into action at twenty yard intervals from the pivot gun, in a straight line. The rudimentary command post was set up behind the gun line or to a flank. Fire orders from the battery's own O.P. were sent in a form that could be directly applied to the gun sights, but map co-ordinates of targets received through the artillery communications network could be converted into 'gun data' by the command post staff, using an artillery board, on which both gun position and target were plotted and bearing and range could thus be deduced.

[17]

Plate 14 *The 18-pdr. limber and wagon. Top – The carriage (i.e., gun) limber open to show storage for 24 rounds of ammunition. The steel doors to both limber and ammunition wagon unfold to reach the ground and provide some measure of protection to the gunners from bullets and splinters. Bottom – The ammunition wagon, which carried 38 rounds. It was pulled behind a limber similar to the carriage limber, but carrying 38 rounds rather than 24, and was the normal source of ready-use ammunition in action.* (Royal Artillery Institution)

The guns were organised in sections of two, each commanded by a subaltern officer known as the 'section commander'. He was responsible for command and supervision of his section in action and for its training in peace-time but was also qualified to work as G.P.O. or as a forward observation officer as necessity arose. A sub-section consisted of one gun (6-horse team, limber and gun with detachment) and its associated ammunition wagons (two at war establishment – often only one for training). These first-line wagons were attached to a limber similar to that used with the gun and pulled by a 6-horse team, so that in the event of casualties there was plenty of spare gun-pulling power. Guns travelled with one ammunition wagon under immediate command and this wagon was dropped beside the gun as part of the drill for coming into action. As it became exhausted, the next wagon was brought on to the position and the first taken away for replenishment. The gun limber carried a certain amount of

[18]

Plate 15 *Ordnance Q.F. 4.5-in. Howitzer Mk.I on Carriage Mk.I. An elevation of 45° could be obtained thanks to the box trail. This enabled the 35-pound shell to be fired to a maximum range of 7,300 yards. (Royal Artillery Institution)*

ammunition but, contrary to modern misconception, in horse-drawn units this was used only in emergency. Gun teams and wagons not required on the gun position were withdrawn to the wagon lines – an area well away from the gun position, giving some protection from counter-battery fire. The wagon lines were commanded by the battery captain, the only captain on the establishment, who was in signal communication with the gun position and could supervise immediate resupply of ammunition, etc.

As the smallest artillery unit organised and equipped to function independently, the battery held its own administrative and repair personnel – gun fitters, farriers and shoeing-smiths, saddlers, wheelers, cooks, clerks, etc. Those who were not at any given time actually working on the gun position were normally grouped in a battery administrative area even further away than the wagon lines and under the local command of the battery quartermaster- [19]

QF 4·5 HOWITZER
CARRIAGE LIMBER

QF 4·5 How.
WAGON

Plate 16
*The 4.5-in.
howitzer limber
and wagon.
Top – The carriage
limber, which had
storage capacity for
12 rounds and was
capable of seating
three members of
the detachment.*
Bottom – *The
ammunition
wagon, which
carried 32 rounds
and could, if
required, seat three
gunners.*
(Royal Artillery
Institution)

sergeant. Here, too, would be found the essential 'cart, cooks' and 'cart, water' that soon found their way on to the battery's own establishment after mobilisation, and the '2nd line' transport provided by the Divisional Train, Army Service Corps. These three general service or 'G.S.' wagons, two for "baggage, stores and supplies" and one for "extra forage", were each pulled by two heavy draught horses. Though they were never detailed on the establishment, it was not uncommon for batteries to add improvised officers' mess carts or forge carts to their administrative train.

The function of the brigade ammunition column was to bring forward ammunition from the divisional dump to battery ammunition points, where it was transferred to the guns' ammunition wagons. Territorial brigades were required to provide all the transport for their brigade ammunition columns by requisitioning on mobilisation to fill 'vacancies' for twelve 4-horse wagons for gun ammunition and nine 4-horse wagons and seven 2-horse carts for small arms ammunition. (An artillery brigade ammunition column was responsible not only for the supply of gun ammunition to the batteries of its own brigade, but also for small arms ammunition to the four battalions of the infantry brigade to which it was affiliated.) By June 1915, the war establishment had been changed, and, it may be presumed, the civilian wagons replaced, so that brigade ammunition columns each had twelve 6-horse general service wag-

[20]

Plate 17
A troublesome Australian-bred remount floored for shoeing by farriers of 270 Brigade, R.F.A., Palestine, 1917. A farrier-sergeant and four shoeing-smiths were on the establishment of each battery and a sergeant of the Army Veterinary Corps was attached.
(Regimental Collection)

ons for gun ammunition and six general service wagons and seven 2-horse carts for small arms ammunition. The general service wagons were later replaced by ammunition wagons and the 2-horse carts by 2-horse limbered general service wagons. Experience in war indicated that ammunition supply needed to be placed under divisional, rather than brigade, control and brigade ammunition columns were removed from the establishment of field artillery brigades and concentrated as divisional ammunition columns. The date on which this change took place varied according to the theatre; in Egypt it was among the measures taken during the lull between the Second and Third Battles of Gaza in the summer of 1917. [21]

Plate 18   *A water cart, not of Government pattern and therefore presumably requisitioned on mobilisation, in use with 1st/2nd Hertfordshire Battery, July 1915.* (Watford Library)

Plate 19   *In the horse lines of 1st/1st Hertfordshire Battery, Egypt, 1916.*
Top left – *Sergeant Peters on a riding horse. There were 44 riding horses on the establishment of a 4-gun battery.*
Top right – *'Buchanan', a draught horse that came out from England with the battery.*
Centre right – *A new addition to the strength. The B.S.M. makes friends with a foal. Its mother, a chestnut mare, is harnessed to a heavy timber sledge but it is not clear whether this was a training aid or a means of smoothing the sandy surface.*
Bottom right – *'Picaninni', evidently heavier than the normal gun- or wagon draught horse and possibly one of those provided by the 54th Divisional Train to pull G.S. wagons.*   (Regimental Collection)

PLATE I   A corporal of the Royal Field Artillery, Territorial Force in walking-out dress, 1910
*(Detail from a chromolithograph after Richard Simkin first published with the Boy's Own Paper of
1st October 1910, reproduced by kind permission of the National Army Museum)*

Walking-out dress was authorised for issue to other ranks of the Territorial Force between 1908 and 1914. The pattern adopted throughout the Royal Field Artillery consisted of a dark blue serge patrol jacket with scarlet collar, brass grenade collar badge and battery shoulder titles, overalls with scarlet stripe, and Royal Artillery-pattern peaked forage cap with brass gun badge. Sergeants and above wore gold lace, corporals and below yellow worsted braid. Although officially described as 'walking-out dress', this uniform was sometimes worn on parade, in addition to its use off duty in mess or while walking out.

Chapter 3

The Early Years, 1908–1914

The Batteries come into being

Hertfordshire Territorial Force Association, founded under the Territorial and Reserve Forces Act, 1907 to administer Territorial units raised in the county, held its inaugural meeting in London on 31st January 1908. After taking steps to fully constitute the Association and to co-opt additional members and appoint a secretary, the meeting turned to the important question of the draft scheme for Hertfordshire's contribution to the Territorial Force that had previously been issued by the War Office. It envisaged that the county would provide two units, to be formed from the existing Hertfordshire Imperial Yeomanry and the 1st and 2nd (Hertfordshire) Volunteer Battalions of the Bedfordshire Regiment, and the greater part of a third unit which would form part of the Royal Field Artillery and would, for practical purposes, be newly raised. The proposed '2nd East Anglian Brigade, Royal Field Artillery' would have its headquarters at Hertford. Two batteries would be raised in Hertfordshire – 1st Hertfordshire Battery, with headquarters at Hertford, would recruit in the east of the county, while 2nd Hertfordshire Battery would cover the west, with headquarters at St. Albans. The brigade ammunition column would also be formed in Hertfordshire, with headquarters at Watford, while the third battery would not be usefully adjacent, perhaps at Luton, but as far away as Peterborough, then in Northamptonshire.

Lacking the courage, and to a certain extent the knowledge, required to approve or reject the scheme, the Association delayed its decision, resolving only "that the two battalions in the county be amalgamated as from the appointed day (*1st April 1908*) but that all other arrangements be deferred until it appear what number of men will take on under the new conditions". At their second meeting, on 6th March 1908, however, the Association were sufficiently confident to approve the scheme and to confirm that they would encourage existing members of the 1st and 2nd Volunteer Battalions to transfer either to the new infantry battalion (soon to be designated 1st Battalion The Hertfordshire Regiment) or to the Royal Field Artillery.

The full detail of the peace establishment of the brigade headquarters, batteries and ammunition column that Hertfordshire was expected to raise was published on 20th March 1908. Brigade headquarters was small – in essence only the personal staff of the commanding officer – for the batteries were self-supporting from the point-of-view of administration and supply. Each battery, of four 15-pdr. B.L.C. guns (see Chapter 2) and eight first-line ammunition wagons, had an establishment of 145 officers and men and 126 horses. The brigade ammunition column – a further twelve wagons – required 158 officers and men and 146 horses. The transfer of the two Volunteer battalions to the Royal Field Artillery as well as to the new infantry battalion was confirmed at the same time, but the designation of the brigade was now shown as '3rd East Anglian', with no change in the battery titles.

The three batteries were formally constituted, and thus able to begin enlistment, at different times. The 1st Northamptonshire Battery, benefitting from the specific transfer of the two Peterborough companies from the 1st Volunteer Battalion The Northamptonshire Regiment, took the lead. According to Stanley (see Bibliography), four officers and about sixty non-commissioned officers and men transferred from the infantry. They were immediately supplemented by a handful of former members of the 1st Northamptonshire Volunteer Engineers, and new enlistments began at once. The transfer of the officers was not announced in the *London Gazette* until 8th September 1908, but with an effective date of 1st April.

Meanwhile, in Hertfordshire things were a little slower. The response of the local Volunteer infantrymen to the call to join the Gunners was much less marked. Only one officer, [23]

Plate 20 *Two experimental other ranks' shoulder titles made for Hertfordshire T.F. Association before application to continue the 'traditional spelling' of the county title was refused by the Army Council. The example on the right would not, in any case, have been approved, since it did not conform to the pattern laid down in Territorial Force Regulations.*
(Regimental Collection)

Captain O.R. McMullen, transferred to 1st Hertfordshire Battery with an effective date of 19th May, announced in the *London Gazette* of 10th November 1908. The same gazette announced the appointment of three new subaltern officers – one for 1st Herts Battery and two for 2nd Herts. Efforts to recruit rank and file were made throughout the county during May and June 1908, with meetings held in several of the larger towns. Typically, on 18th May the secretary of Hertfordshire Territorial Force Association, Lieutenant-Colonel Gripper, took the chair at the meeting held in Hertford Town Hall. After describing the background to the new Territorial units, Colonel Gripper explained that recruits would have to do 45 drills in their first year of service and that "they would readily understand that number would be necessary for beginners because there was more to learn than had been the case in the past with the infantry". At a similar meeting held at Hatfield a few days earlier, fifteen or sixteen people had given in their names as willing to enlist and thirty or so indicated willingness at the Hertford meeting. Half the battery ("about seventy") would serve at Hertford, which included a detachment at Hatfield, with the other half at St. Albans. In its report of this meeting, the *Hertfordshire Mercury* records that Colonel Gripper had said that the 1st Herts Battery was not yet able to enlist men (hence the compiling of a list of volunteers) but that since the meeting authority to do so had been received. The receipt of this authority appears to coincide with the effective date of Captain McMullen's transfer – 19th May 1908 – which, in all probability, is the 'birthday' of Gunner units raised in Hertfordshire.

The question of uniform for the new brigade had by now been under consideration for some weeks, and Colonel Gripper announced at the meeting at Hertford that service dress would be "as for the Royal Field Artillery" but that the pattern of walking-out dress had not yet been decided. In fact, Territorial Associations had no latitude in the matter of service dress and probably very little as far as walking-out dress was concerned, either. The Hertfordshire Association made an interesting, but historically ill-founded, attempt to have the county name spelt 'Hartfordshire' when applied to local units. At their meeting on 27th April 1908, they resolved to seek authority for this spelling from the War Office, and even went so far as to have two sample shoulder titles made for the Hertfordshire batteries. One of these did not

Plate 21 *The gilding metal shoulder title approved for wear by other ranks of 1st and 2nd Hertfordshire Batteries in service dress and in walking-out dress.*
Actual size 2 in. × 1¾ in. (Regimental Collection)

conform to the pattern laid down in *Territorial Force Regulations* and by 6th July 1908, when the Association next met, it was clear that neither gained War Office approval as to spelling, for a curt reply had been received that the spelling 'Hertfordshire' was to be used, "abbreviated when necessary as Herts". Specimens of the sample titles have survived and are illustrated, together with the authorised pattern, at Plates 20 and 21. There is no indication that Northamptonshire had any such difficulty in accepting the prescribed title 'T. – R.F.A. – NORTHANTS'.

It had not been the custom, prior to transfer to the Territorial Force, for Volunteer units to wear gold lace or gilt badges on their full-dress uniforms and it may well have been assumed that the Territorial artillery would wear silver or white metal rather than gilt or brass. However, a number of new units applied for permission to wear gold lace and their consolidated petition was submitted to the King on 22nd October 1908:

> "That Your Majesty may be graciously pleased to approve of those units of the Territorial Force detailed in the accompanying memorandum being permitted to adopt gold lace and gilt ornaments instead of silver lace and white metal ornaments.
>
> The memorandum explains in each case the special reasons put forward in support of the request, and the County Associations concerned are unanimous in the opinion that this concession would favourably influence recruiting."

Both Hertfordshire and Northamptonshire Associations supported the application and gave as their reasons "the unanimous wish of the officers, being new units" and "to popularise the batteries and promote recruiting". The submission was approved and officers and men were able to adopt uniform and badges similar to those worn by their Regular counterparts. The only significant difference, which would have required close examination before it became apparent, was the substitution of a laurel sprig for the honour '*Ubique*' on the upper scroll of the cap badge (see page 5).

With the colour of their lace and 'ornaments' – in this case badges, buttons and shoulder titles – fixed, the way was now clear for the unit and the two Associations to put forward their proposals for walking-out dress, They chose to conform to orthodox Gunner patterns for all ranks, though it is by no means clear whether they had any choice. Officers seem, from the few photographs available, to have worn the blue patrol jacket ('frock, serge, universal') with overalls, peaked forage cap and Sam Browne belt – a much plainer and less colourful uniform than that specified for other ranks. Photographs show that they were issued with a tunic which most closely resembles Campbell's description (see Bibliography) of the other ranks' patrol jacket (or 'frock') introduced in 1878. The new tunic had seven buttons down the front, rather than five, but other major features – the scarlet collar with grenade badge, shoulder straps on which titles were worn, and the use of yellow worsted braid around the collar and in the cuff decoration, with sergeants and above having gold braid – follow the 1878 pattern. It is evident from photographs (Plates 24 and 26) that the Austrian knot was used as cuff decoration, rather than the 'crow's foot' quoted by Campbell. This dark blue tunic was worn with scarlet-striped overalls and Royal Artillery-pattern peaked forage cap with brass gun badge. The most striking part of the uniform, though, which does not show up well on the photographic plates of the time, was the R.F.A.-pattern web girdle, worn as a waist belt. The girdle had stripes of ½-in. scarlet, ½-in. blue, ¼-in. yellow, ½-in. blue, ½-in. scarlet, presenting an appearance similar to that of the present-day Royal Artillery stable belt.

A Sound Foundation – Recruiting and Training, 1908–1910

At the Hertfordshire Association's meeting on 6th July 1908, the strength, as at 30th June, of the two Hertfordshire batteries and the ammunition column was given as five officers and 119 men out of an establishment of fifteen officers and 433 men. It is known, however, that less than a dozen men had so far joined the ammunition column, so the combined battery strengths would have been very close to the reported strengths, or about 38 per cent of establishment. This figure and Stanley's remarks about the success of recruiting into the Peterborough battery are consistent with the brigade's application late in June, on behalf of all three batteries, for recognition by the Army Council as a formally constituted unit of the Territorial Force (for which an attested strength of at least thirty per cent was required). Recognition "exclusive of ammunition column" was granted by Army Council letter dated

Plate 22   *A gunner of 1st Hertfordshire Battery in khaki service dress. He is wearing the 1903-pattern bandolier, indicating that the photograph was taken after 1910. (Plate 28, taken in 1910, shows the earlier pattern.)*
(Regimental Collection)

2nd July 1908, promulgated by Army Order 198 of 1908, with the unit cited under its original title of 2nd East Anglian Brigade. This title remained in use for only a short time longer – perhaps into August 1908; it had certainly been changed by early September. Hertfordshire Association received a report at its meeting on 12th October, explaining that "artillery brigades in East Anglia have been renumbered following representations by the other brigades. The Herts Brigade, originally allotted the number 2, is in fact the only completely new unit and, in deference to units with former Volunteer Force traditions, will take the last position in the order of precedence and will be numbered 4". It was not necessary to change the designations of the batteries.

Matters of uniform and title may have seemed rather remote as the newly-formed batteries struggled to find and appoint key personnel, especially officers, and to put in some preparatory training prior to the first annual camp, to be held in August. In Hertfordshire, and doubtless in Northamptonshire too, local newspapers were helpful in publishing a condensed but readily understandable form of battery routine orders, as, for instance, in the *Hertfordshire Mercury* of 18th July 1908 – "1st Herts Battery, R.F.A. – Drill: Monday for gunners and drivers at Drill Hall; Wednesday and Thursday for gunners and drivers at Port Vale Meadow, 6.30 p.m."

The brigade's first annual camp took place at Shoeburyness, in Essex, during the first fortnight of August, 1908, with all four East Anglian brigades attending. The Hertfordshire batteries mustered just over eighty and thirty men respectively, but with only two officers each – Captain O.R. McMullen and 2nd Lieutenant J. Urban Smith in 1st Herts Battery and 2nd Lieutenants E.A.H. Bailey and G.R. Holland in 2nd Herts. Stanley records that the Peterborough battery went to camp with a strength of more than one hundred. No commanding officer had yet been appointed and Lieutenant-Colonel J.T. Woolrych Perowne, officer commanding 1st Northants Battery took command of the brigade during camp. The fortnight seems to have started on rather a relaxing note, for after inspecting the brigade and [26] outlining camp routine at 10.00 a.m. on Sunday, 2nd August, Colonel Woolrych Perowne

Plate 23 *A gunner of 1st Hertfordshire Battery wearing the mounted-pattern greatcoat.*   (Regimental Collection)

"dismissed the men for the rest of the day, and a large number of them paid a visit to Southend" (*Hertfordshire Mercury*). Gun and driving drill and semaphore practice occupied the whole of the next two days and on Wednesday the gunners were "taken to the barracks and had practice at firing at targets out to sea". This was good progress for the newly-formed batteries and it was reported that "considering that it was the first time they had fired, they did very well". A similar static practice took place on Saturday, then on the Wednesday of the second week, "the men paraded at 5.00 a.m. and at 6.30 they were marched to a point about two miles out of town, being accompanied by the horse teams for the guns and ammunition wagons, and were given practice at firing at invisible targets, the guns firing over a high bank by means of a dial sight, the object being to test the shooting of the men while under cover". Tactical drills "in the open field, going into action, etc." took up the remaining two days.

Competitions, a feature of annual camp in the Volunteer Force, naturally continued after the change to the Territorial Force and the batteries began to assemble the usual collection of cups for gun drill, gun laying, best turned-out gun and team, etc. In the first gun-laying competition between 1st and 2nd Herts Batteries, held at Shoeburyness, 2nd Herts Battery won handsomely. (Five of their six representative layers, the *Watford Observer* pointed out, were employed at Watford Post Office.) Press reports of the end of camp were enthusiastic. The brigade had "spent a pleasant and profitable time at Shoeburyness"; the health of the men had been good; general satisfaction had been expressed at the arrangements in camp and the men had had "ample practice in firing . . . and the opinion formed by Colonel Massey, who was in command of the camp, was very favourable". An excellent start had indeed been made in less than six months but there was much to be done, as the brigade's first year progressed, to consolidate and build upon the successes. The ammunition column, for instance, had not yet been formed; more officers, including a commanding officer, were required; issues of guns and wagons had yet to be completed; and horses had to be 'enlisted', or at least made available for local training in the battery areas.

[27]

Plate 24   *Gunner Saville of 1st Hertfordshire Battery in blue walking-out dress, c.1912. The T. – R.F.A. – Herts shoulder title can be distinguished. The collar is scarlet, edged with yellow braid. The knot above the cuff is also in yellow braid but the photographic plate was not properly sensitive to yellow light* (see Plate 26).

(Regimental Collection)

At its meeting on 12th October 1908, Hertfordshire Territorial Association received a report that the Hertfordshire batteries' headquarters and outlying drill stations were now established as follows:

	Headquarters	*Drill Stations*
1st Hertfordshire Battery	Hertford	St. Albans
		Hatfield
		Harpenden
2nd Hertfordshire Battery	Watford	Hemel Hempstead
		Berkhamsted
		Tring
		Kings Langley

The Peterborough battery did not open any outlying drill stations at once. They took over the drill hall that had belonged to G and H Companies of the 1st Volunteer Battalion The Northamptonshire Regiment and it was altered to suit artillery requirements. In addition, according to Stanley, "a gun shed and harness room were built in the yard of Messrs. Sexton, Grimwade and Beck's repository". The report that the ammunition column was based at 'Royston or Watford' was at best premature, at worst simply wishful thinking. The Hertfordshire Association resolutely rejected a proposal from Huntingdonshire that responsibility for raising the ammunition column should be transferred to that county, while continuing to discuss how it could best be located within the brigade area. Royston was favoured by the Association but little seems to have happened before their next meeting on 21st December. Here, they heard that the G.O.C. East Anglian Division had endorsed their decision that the ammunition column should not be located in Huntingdonshire. An interesting new suggestion, which had been briefly discussed in October, was presented to the December meeting on behalf of C.R.A. East Anglian Division. He suggested that sections of the ammunition column should be raised in the three battery centres, where they would form what would today be

Plate 25   *Lieutenant-Colonel R.M. Foot, Commanding Officer of 4th East Anglian Brigade, R.F.A. from February 1909 to January 1914. Colonel Foot, of Berkhamsted, retired from the Royal Inniskilling Fusiliers after seventeen years' service in 1902. After a very short period in command of 2nd Hertfordshire Battery, he was selected to command 4th East Anglian Brigade, and did so for the five very important formative years leading up to the First World War. On relinquishing command of the brigade, he reverted to the Regular Army Reserve of Officers, from which he was recalled in August 1914 to serve with great distinction in staff appointments in France.* (Photograph taken c.1919) (Regimental Collection)

called a 'basic training wing'. Recruits would enlist into the ammunition column and transfer to the battery proper only when fully trained. The Association resolved that the decision should await the appointment of the brigade's first commanding officer. Eventually, after a proposal to recruit the whole of the column in Northamptonshire had been discarded, sections were raised with each battery, though it is not clear whether the C.R.A.'s plan for their use for basic training was fully put into effect. It was not until May 1910 that the two Hertfordshire sections of the column had attested the necessary thirty per cent of establishment and achieved Army Council recognition (Army Order 166 of 1910), and recognition of the Northamptonshire section was not promulgated until January 1911 (Army Order 39 of 1911). Captain S.G. Cook transferred from the Peterborough battery to command the ammunition column and the first two subaltern officers were commissioned on 1st June and 1st October 1910, for service with the Northamptonshire and Hertfordshire sections, respectively. (The ammunition column was established with four sections, three of which were concerned with the supply of artillery ammunition to the three batteries of the 4th East Anglian Brigade, while the fourth supplied small arms ammunition to the infantry battalions with which the batteries were working.) Although it is known that the batteries, which had been issued with only one gun each before camp, received the balance of guns and all their ammunition wagons during September, it is not clear whether the full establishment of wagons was issued to the ammunition column, which was in any case strictly limited in the number of wagons and horses it could take to annual camp. Information is sparse but it does seem that the ammunition column may have been rather a 'Cinderella' in comparison with the batteries.

Captain McMullen, who had so successfully led 1st Hertfordshire Battery through its formative stages, was promoted to major in November 1908, with his seniority backdated to 19th May, the date of his original transfer from the infantry. At the same time, it looked as if the search for a suitable commander for 2nd Hertfordshire Battery had at last proved successful. Major R.M. Foot, of White Hill, Berkhamsted, a retired Regular officer of the Royal Inniskilling Fusiliers and former adjutant of 2nd (Hertfordshire) Volunteer Battalion The Bedfordshire Regiment, was persuaded to join the Territorial Artillery and was appointed to command 2nd Hertfordshire Battery with effect from 10th November 1908. Within a matter of weeks, however, Major Foot was selected as the first commanding officer of 4th East Anglian Brigade and he was promoted lieutenant-colonel on 17th February 1909. Lieutenant-Colonel Foot's appointment as commanding officer coincided with the appointment as Honorary Colonel of [29]

Plate 26 *The warrant officers and senior non-commissioned officers of 2nd Hertfordshire Battery at annual camp in 1910. Standing (L.–R.) Fitter-Sgt. James, B.S.M. Coles, Sgt. Smith, Sgt. Mowberry, Sgt. Wingfield, Farrier Staff-Sgt. Butcher, B.Q.M.S. Jones, Sgt. Reeves. Seated (L.–R.) B.S.M. Howes, R.S.M. Rees, B.S.M. Conelly (P.S.I.s).* (Regimental Collection)

4th East Anglian Brigade of Colonel The Marquess of Salisbury, C.B., A.D.C., who had served with the Hertfordshire Yeomanry Cavalry from 1880 to 1887, when he transferred to the Hertfordshire Militia (4th Battalion The Bedfordshire Regiment), which he commanded with great distinction in South Africa. The brigade's first adjutant, Captain J.C. Dunbar, R.F.A., had been appointed with effect from 1st September 1908.

The question of how the Hertfordshire sub-units were to have access to the necessary horses for local training and for annual camp was addressed by Hertfordshire Association early in 1909. One horse (whether draught or riding is not specified in the minutes) had been presented to 1st Herts Battery soon after the first annual camp, but to field four guns and the battery staff for, e.g., local week-end training, required between 50–60 horses. The Association accordingly agreed, in response to the recommendations of a special sub-committee, and bearing in mind the considerable difficulty that had been encountered in obtaining suitable horses for training, to provide twelve horses for each battery at approximately £35 each. A standing 'Horse Committee' was established, consisting initially of Colonel Foot, Major McMullen, Captain Dunbar and the Association secretary, and the sum of £840 was voted for the purpose. An agreement was drawn up under which local farmers and tradesmen would provide 'board and lodging' for Association horses and would have the use of the horses except when they were required for local training, which was restricted to twice a week, and for annual camp. By the beginning of April 1909 fifteen horses had been bought at rather less than £35 each and the Horse Committee continued their work of supervising provision of 'Association horses' until mobilisation in 1914. The core of Association horses was, of course, supplemented by a few horses that belonged to members of the batteries and by others that were borrowed from local firms, notably the breweries. It was normal in Regular batteries for the draught horses to be carefully matched in pairs and for them to work in the same place in the team (lead, centre or wheel) and under the same driver – a system hardly available to the Territorials, who were dependent on the men and animals available for a given evening or week-end and had to make the best of those who turned up. (Present-day Territorials will recognise yet another case of *'plus ça change, plus c'est la même chose'*!).

Another difficulty, which would certainly not occur to the present-day driver, was caused [30] by the harness first issued to the batteries. Although Regular batteries had adopted breast-harness for draught teams in 1902, the newly formed Territorial batteries had to make do with neck-collar harness of a pattern introduced in the 1860's. Neck-collars had to be fitted to individual horses and this led Hertfordshire Association, at the request of the brigade, to approach the War Office with the resolution that, "Neck-collar draught harness is not suitable for Territorial Royal Field Artillery, since the same horses cannot always be obtained". The secretary was directed to enquire whether breast-harness could be considered. The reply, received in time for the Association meeting on 11th January 1909, stated that breast-harness could not be considered, whereupon the Association began to debate whether funds could be provided for the alteration of the neck-collar harness to the breast-pattern. There is no record of whether such alterations were undertaken, or indeed when breast-harness was issued. All that is evident is that breast-harness was in use at the time the batteries were mobilised in 1914.

In 1909, annual camp was held at Lydd, in Kent, during the last week of July and the first week of August, the batteries travelling by special train to arrive on Sunday afternoon. The first firing practice took place on the Wednesday of the first week, with the next three days occupied by 'fire and manoeuvre' exercises. Church parade on the 'middle Sunday' was at Lydd church and "the men looked very smart in their blue uniforms", according to the *Hertfordshire Mercury*. Colonel Massey, C.R.A. East Anglian Division, inspected the brigade during the second week. The *Hertfordshire Mercury* correspondent witnessed the inspection and commented on the "fine sight when the batteries of the 4th East Anglian Brigade, consisting of twelve guns and the same number of wagons are manoeuvred about in close order", concluding that the drills had "passed off successfully and to the credit of those taking part". The batteries travelled home on Sunday – an unusual arrangement which attracted no comment in the press but is unlikely to have been popular with those, probably the great majority, who would have to have been back at their civilian jobs early the following morning.

As the year 1910 opened, Hertfordshire Association were awaiting War Office approval of a proposal made by Colonel Foot in October 1909 that "both for efficiency and the convenience of the men" the left half-battery of 2nd Herts Battery should move from Hemel Hempstead to concentrate with the right half-battery at Watford. Approval was recorded at the Association meeting on 17th January 1910 and the move was put into effect. The expression "for the convenience of the men" suggests that the great majority of the battery was recruited in the immediate area of Watford, rather than across a broader sweep of western Hertfordshire, as had originally been anticipated. It is probable that the drill stations at Hemel Hempstead and Berkhamsted were closed, though with the co-operation of the Hertfordshire Regiment it may have been possible for the battery to keep a toe-hold in these towns that would have been useful on winter evenings when a journey to Watford was less appealing. Concentration of 1st Hertfordshire Battery took place the following year. Perhaps surprisingly, the right half-battery moved from Hertford to St. Albans following Association approval, based on "strong representations" by Headquarters East Anglian Division. Curiously, at the very time that the batteries in Hertfordshire were concentrating in the larger towns, the Peterborough battery was, according to Stanley, opening, though possibly unofficially, an outlying station at Stamford, across the border into Lincolnshire. The ammunition column eventually declared its headquarters to be with Brigade Headquarters at Hertford, though sections seem still to have been recruited in the battery areas, and by 1912 the layout of the brigade had stabilised and was shown in the *Monthly Army List* as:

Brigade Headquarters	28 St. Andrew Street, Hertford
1st Hertfordshire Battery	Harpenden Road, St. Albans
2nd Hertfordshire Battery	Clarendon Hall, Watford
1st Northamptonshire Battery	Queen's Street, Peterborough
Brigade Ammunition Column	28 St. Andrew Street, Hertford

Annual camp was at Lydd again in 1910, and once more with one week in July and one in August. The routine was by now well established – the batteries travelled by special train to arrive on Saturday, spent a day unpacking and in general preparation, and after a gentle day's training on Monday undertook more complicated and more active exercises. The *Hertfordshire Mercury* correspondent was again with the brigade and noted following Tuesday's training that, "the admirable manner in which the horses were managed and operations carried out reflected great credit on the drivers and their instructor, B.S.M. Young". The following day the brigade "again engaged in field operations" and the "excellent way in which all concerned

The Herts Bat: in Action – Note Recoil of N ^{o} 1 Gun. 1280.

Plate 27   *2nd Hertfordshire Battery in action with borrowed 15-pdr. B.L.C. guns during the final of the King's Cup competition at Okehampton, Devon in August 1910. No. 1 gun, nearest the camera, has just fired and the barrel and breech can be seen at full recoil.*
(Regimental Collection)

carried out their work was very evident". The G.O.C.-in-C. Eastern Command inspected the divisional artillery (all four East Anglian brigades were in camp) on Thursday and was reported to be "well pleased with what he had seen and with the smart appearance". Musketry practice took place on the middle Saturday – the first time it had been noticed in the *Mercury's* report of camp – with church parade, in blue uniform, on Sunday morning. The second week began with a hard day's work on Monday and then on Tuesday, "The brigade was called upon at a moment's notice to turn out in field service marching order and proceed to Shorncliffe – a distance of eighteen miles. Equipment was hurriedly packed and men and guns were on the road in a very short time. This order was a test one and was admirably carried out. The men returned the following day, about noon". The prospect of a fortnight by the seaside in the summer was, of course, a significant factor in persuading many young men to join the Territorials and this year they must have been content with their decision to sign on, for the weather at camp was exceptionally hot and gave the men "the appearance of seasoned campaigners". The Hertford detachment did not arrive home until 11.30 p.m. on the final
[32] Sunday, reportedly "tired out", for the whole training had been "very vigorous".

Plate 28   *Officers and men of 2nd Hertfordshire Battery, winners of the King's Cup competition for Territorial field batteries in 1910. Captain G.R. Holland, commanding the battery, is seated, centre.*   (Regimental Collection)

The King's Cup, 1910

The vigorous training paid off before the end of August, to the great credit of 2nd Herts Battery, who had qualified at Lydd to take part in the year's final competition for the King's Cup, organised by the National Artillery Association. The final was due to be held on the Okehampton ranges in Devon on Thursday 25th August. Captain G.R. Holland, commanding the battery, two subaltern officers and sixty men managed to get additional time off work in order to take part and they travelled the previous day by special train, arriving late in the evening. Weather conditions on Thursday prevented the completion of the day's programme and several batteries had to fire on the Friday, the draw placing 2nd Herts Battery last-but-one in the order of competition, at 3.00 p.m. Guns and ammunition wagons and their teams were provided from Regular Army sources, with the result that competing batteries had the additional problem of unfamiliarity, especially with the horses. The *Watford Observer* described the competition thus:

"Before coming into action the battery waited at a given spot for its orders. A staff officer of the Regular Army brought these to the battery commander and immediately the 2nd Herts got to work. After horsing the guns, which was done with the utmost smartness, they were taken to some cover. The idea of the contest is that the battery is firing at an enemy who cannot see them, and any movement which exposes it to view is heavily penalised by loss of marks. The enemy was a row of dummy infantry, the distance being given approximately as from 2,700 to 4,000 yards. The actual distance of the target from the battery was nearly 4,000 yards – well over two miles. Range-takers found the distance and firing commenced with shrapnel. Thirty-two rounds of ammunition were allowed to each gun for ranging and effect. Six of these rounds were used for getting the range, and in a very short time the 2nd Herts were doing grand execution amongst the enemy. The effect of the firing was watched by men stationed in bomb-proof shelters near the targets. To make an effective hit with this kind of ammunition the shell has to be directed to a spot about one hundred yards in front of the target; one bursting over the dummies themselves hardly does any damage. While the battery were at work all their actions were closely observed by the chief judge, Colonel Smith, commandant of the Okehampton range, and other officers of the Regular Army. These men were on the look-out for points in firing, effect, discipline, driving, manoeuvring, drill, quietness, orderly work, reconnoitring for position and range-taking, all of which had to be considered in giving a decision. After the firing the battery took their horses back very smartly and once again formed into position."

The Watford battery were declared winners with the splendid score of 82½ per cent, the runners-up scoring 63½ per cent. This was clearly a triumph, and the first time that one of the newly-formed Territorial batteries had won the King's Prize. The winners in both 1908 and 1909 were 1st Hampshire Battery, from Portsmouth, who had Volunteer experience as a garrison battery. The cup, of ornate design and in solid silver, was accompanied by a silver badge for each man who took part, and money prizes totalling £35. The *Watford Observer* congratulated all concerned, especially Sergeant Howes and Sergeant Connelly, the battery's two permanent-staff-instructors, recording that "a small but enthusiastic company greeted the victors on their return to Watford soon after midnight on Friday", and at the same time forecasting that, "at a more favourable hour and on a more fitting occasion, Watford will be able to voice . . . congratulations". The people of Watford did indeed find the appropriate time, place and means of congratulating the battery, which they did by the gift of a large and very handsome silver cup. The King's Prize, 1910 and the Watford Cup are among the principal pieces of silver in the hands of 2nd Hertfordshire Battery's present-day successors.

Prelude to Active Service, 1911–1914

The year 1910 closed with the batteries respectably, but not fully, recruited, each needing between 20–30 men to reach establishment. The ammunition column, too, was making progress, and the Hertfordshire component reported a strength of two officers and 76 men against an establishment of three officers and 102 men. Early the following year, Hertfordshire Association approved plans for providing horses on mobilisation. Horses were not formally 'enlisted' in peacetime and Hertfordshire would have needed to find about four hundred for brigade headquarters, two batteries and two sections of the ammunition column, in addition to at least that number for the Hertfordshire Yeomanry. As far as can be established, no steps were taken to prevent other units, and especially the Remount Service, from scouring the countryside for horses, including those earmarked for local units, and although the Hertfordshire Association had conscientiously attempted to ensure that their own units were properly horsed on mobilisation, the plan did not, unfortunately, work when put into practice in 1914.

The coronation of Their Majesties King George V and Queen Mary took place at Westminster Abbey on 22nd June 1911. Territorial brigades of the Royal Field Artillery were required to find a party consisting of one officer and seventeen non-commissioned officers and men for street-lining duties on the processional route. These parties paraded for practice on 21st June, then for the street lining itself, which lasted from 8.00 a.m. until mid-afternoon on Coronation Day, and again for Their Majesties' drive round the streets of London on 23rd June. Accommodation was arranged in camps set up in the London parks. The custom of the Sovereign awarding a medal to commemorate such events as coronations or jubilees was by now established and King George V's Coronation Medal was awarded on a scale of four medals to each Territorial brigade of the Royal Field Artillery. Following a laid-down formula, within 4th East Anglian Brigade these medals went to the commanding officer (Lieutenant-Colonel R.M. Foot), the officer commanding the street-lining detachment (Captain G.R. Holland, 2nd Herts Battery), the senior warrant officer or non-commissioned officer (B.S.M. W. Barker, 1st Herts Battery) and a gunner selected by the commanding officer (Gunner E. Flintoft, 1st Northants Battery). Sergeant-Major Barker had transferred to 1st Herts Battery from 1st Volunteer Battalion The Bedfordshire Regiment and it was through service with the battalion that he had qualified for the Volunteer Long Service Medal presented to him at camp in 1909, to which he now added the Coronation Medal. His seniority within the brigade was very evident – he held regimental number 1!

The Volunteer Officers' Decoration and the Volunteer Long Service Medal were replaced in 1909 by similar awards for efficient service in the Territorial Force – the Territorial Decoration, for twenty years' commissioned service and the Territorial Force Efficiency Medal for twelve years' service in the ranks. Earlier efficient service in the Volunteer Force was recognised as qualifying service for the new awards, which were made in small numbers to officers and men of 4th East Anglian Brigade between 1910 and mobilisation in 1914. Major O.R. McMullen was the only officer to receive the Territorial Decoration and there were less than a dozen awards of the medal. Amendments to the regulations for both awards, providing for embodied service to count double, were promulgated after the war, as a result of which the Territorial Decoration was awarded to four more officers and the medal to some fifty other ranks. (For details see *Hertfordshire Yeomanry and Artillery Honours and Awards*.)

As annual camp, 1911 approached, local newspapers continued to provide a suitable means of disseminating battery routine orders. The following is quoted in full from the *Watford Observer*:

2nd Herts Battery, Royal Field Artillery
Battery Orders for week ending 2nd July 1911

by Captain G.R. Holland, R.F.A.(T.)

Drills and Parades

Wednesday 28th June at 8.00 p.m.: All ranks – foot and carbine drill.

Thursday 29th June at 8.00 p.m.: N.C.O.s and gunners – gun drill, laying and fuse setting; drivers – harness cleaning.

Saturday 1st July at 3.00 p.m.: Foot parade and guard of honour at the opening ceremony of the Watford Miniature Rifle Club. Dress – blue uniform. Gunners to carry carbines with slings. N.C.O.s and men who are unable to attend this parade will please notify the instructors as early as possible.

Sunday 2nd July at 1.45 p.m.: Voluntary church parade and procession in aid of the Orphan Fund of the A.S.R.S. (Watford Branch). Dress – blue uniform with white gloves. Squad parade – 1.30 p.m.

Annual Camp

It is notified for information that the annual training will now be held from 30th July to 13th August instead of from 29th July to 12th August.

Drills

N.C.O.s and men who are behind with their attendances at drill are again warned of the necessity of completing the full number of drills required by regulations to be carried out before annual training, viz, Trained men – 20.

> George R. Holland
> Captain, R. F. A. (T.)
> Commanding 2nd Herts Battery, R.F.A.
> Watford, June 21st, 1911.

Similar orders published in the *Hertfordshire Mercury* on 24th June showed that 1st Herts Battery were preparing energetically for camp. There were drills each evening Monday–Friday and on Saturday afternoon. Of particular interest is the remark against the semaphore signalling drill on Friday evening – "all drivers to attend if possible" – evidence, even in those days, of the need for swift and accurate communication between the gun position and the wagon lines.

Some 430 all ranks of the brigade attended annual camp in 1911, during the by now conventional first two weeks of August. For the first time, the training was split between two different places – the first week at Lydd, where firing could take place, and the second week near Thetford in Norfolk. (There was no War Office-controlled training area at Thetford, as there is now, and exercises would have taken place over privately owned land, without, of course, any live firing.) The brigade moved by train to Thetford on the middle Sunday, stopping at Tottenham to water the horses, and reached camp during the evening. A correspondent to the *Hertfordshire Mercury* reported that the ground locally was "very bad for artillery work, rabbit holes being in abundance" and that there were several minor accidents. For what appears to have been the first time, the brigade joined other units in night manoeuvres, "which consisted of divisional operations against a skeleton force". Once again, the batteries travelled home on a Sunday; the Hertford battery did not arrive until 8.45 p.m.

Strength reports for January 1912 showed that the Hertfordshire batteries were at much the same strength as a year previously, needing 25–30 men to reach establishment in each case. There were, however, now only twelve Association horses and growing signs of difficulty in

Plate 29 *A 15-pdr. B.L.C. gun of 1st Northamptonshire Battery, followed by a 4-horse ammunition wagon, in Narrow Street, Peterborough, c.1912. It is not known why the shield has been removed from the gun* (see Plate 10). (Peterborough Museum)

MAYOR & OFFICERS PETERBORO' TERRITORIALS, 1913.

Plate 30 *Officers of local Territorial units with the Mayor of Peterborough, 1913. Two officers of 1st Northamptonshire Battery can be seen on the right of the group, wearing blue patrol uniform with Sam Browne belt.*
(Peterborough Library)

horsing guns and wagons. Comprehensive reports of camp at Larkhill, on Salisbury Plain, were published in both the usual newspapers and included such passages as, "Monday . . . was spent in teaming the horses, which is a very ticklish job, and many exciting scenes were witnessed" (*Hertfordshire Mercury*), followed by, "The horses in training this year are not nearly so good as previously, and this seems to be the most difficult problem the County Association have to face". The *Watford Observer* struck a slightly more romantic note on the same subject:

"A hard task faced the battery when they had settled down in camp, as the draught horses received for gun-team work had to be subdued. Fresh horses are taken every year. The animals, mostly young, very much resented being used for war-like purposes and there was many a tough tussle between man and beast. In a few days the battery were able to start work with very creditable teams of horses."

Live firing began on Wednesday, so the "few days" were in fact less than two; allowance has evidently been made for improvement during the training. Northamptonshire Association seem to have been much more generous in their provision of horses. Although, according to Stanley, they did not start to buy horses until 1911, by 1913 "forty blacks had been acquired and were boarded out with farmers and tradesmen."

The brigade was in camp close to the Military Flying School and the *Watford Observer* recorded that "the men were intensely interested in the aeroplanes", continuing:

"At first horses were rather unsettled at the unusual sight and the noise of the motors, but towards the end of camp had become quite accustomed to them, although at times six machines would be overhead at the same time. On one of the firing days, while the battery were awaiting orders to proceed to action, two aeroplanes drawn up on a small slope just in front of the battery were put in flight at a few seconds' interval. They passed directly over the battery, so close that one seemed able to touch them. The first somewhat startled the horses but the passage of the second machine did not disturb them. In actual warfare the noise of aeroplanes might stampede a battery, and the object of the flight was to test the horses."

Major O.R. McMullen retired from command of 1st Hertfordshire Battery just before camp in 1912. He was succeeded as battery commander by Major G.R.H. Bowden, who transferred from 1st South Midland Brigade, apparently on moving from the Gloucester area to St. Albans. At the same time, Captain G.R. Holland, who had acted as battery commander of 2nd Hertfordshire Battery in the ranks of second lieutenant and captain – he 'leapfrogged' the rank of lieutenant – was promoted to major, and the brigade's first padre, the appropriately named Reverend Alan Chaplin, C.F., Rector of Chesterton, near Peterborough, was appointed in time to conduct his first service at the open-air church parade held on the middle Sunday of camp. In addition to a chaplain, the brigade was entitled to a medical officer. This appointment was

[36]

Plate 31 *A detachment of 1st Northamptonshire Battery providing the gun carriage for a military funeral at Peterborough in 1913. It was very unusual for the blue walking-out uniform to be worn on mounted parades.* (Regimental Collection)

filled in March 1913, when Dr. Josiah Walker, of Peterborough, was commissioned as a lieutenant in the Royal Army Medical Corps (T.F.) and attached to brigade headquarters. Although a veterinary officer was included in both the peace and war establishments of a Territorial artillery brigade, none were 'permanently attached' in peacetime so that, unlike the medical officer and the chaplain, they were not shown in individual brigades' entries in the *Monthly Army List.*

Annual training in 1913 was again a 'split camp'. The first week was spent at Dibgate Camp, Shorncliffe, Kent in company with the four infantry battalions of the East Midland Brigade and a heavy battery, Royal Garrison Artillery. For the first time, the batteries had the opportunity of practising their role in support of infantry, in both attack and defence, though this training was necessarily 'dry', i.e., without live ammunition. The *Watford Observer* passed an interesting comment on the difficulty of movement across the training area, remarking that, "on several occasions as many as ten horses were required to drag a gun up the long and steep hills the battery had to cross". On the Tuesday of the second week, the brigade moved to Lydd for three days' live firing, when "all the theoretical knowledge acquired during the year was put to severe practical tests" and, as far as 2nd Herts Battery were concerned, "the high standard of efficiency and fire discipline shown by the battery in former years was fully maintained". It is clear from the *Watford Observer* report that the handsome 'Watford Challenge Cup' presented after the battery's success in the King's Prize, 1910 was now in use as a 'best sub-section' trophy, apparently with differing competitions each year. At Lydd, the competition took the form of "an alarm turn-out to an appointed rendezvous, marks being given for time, completeness, cleanliness, etc." Unlike the modern alarm race, which is held in an arena, this competition was liable to start at any time during the working day in camp, and so, "shortly after three o'clock, without any previous announcement, Major Holland ordered the turn-out to be sounded, and in nine minutes from the alarm the first sub-section ('A' – Sergeant Humphries) was moving off to the rendezvous, followed at very close intervals by the other sub-sections". This was the more remarkable, since "when the alarm was given several of the men were away on various duties and the drivers were engaged in harness cleaning, several having their harness stripped for that purpose". The batteries reached home rather earlier at the end of camp in 1913. At the expense of reveille at 3.00 a.m., 2nd Herts Battery arrived at Watford station at 10.00 a.m. and "the operation of detraining the horses, guns and wagons was watched with the greatest interest . . . by a large number of spectators".

After very nearly four years in command of 4th East Anglian Brigade, Lieutenant-Colonel Foot retired in January 1914. He was succeeded by Lieutenant-Colonel The Marquess of [37]

Plate 32   *Major The Marquess of Exeter, who was appointed to command 1st Northamptonshire Battery in May 1910. In January 1914 he was promoted to the command of 4th East Anglian Brigade, which he held until February 1917, when he was transferred to command of the Royal Horse Artillery of the Imperial Mounted Division. He is wearing the officers' pattern khaki service dress introduced in 1902, which was replaced by a new pattern, in which the jacket was worn open at the neck with a collar and tie, in 1913. His two ribbons are for the 1902 and 1911 Coronation Medals, both of which he received in a civilian capacity. He was twice mentioned in despatches for services during the First World War and appointed C.M.G. in 1919.*   (Regimental Collection)

Exeter, who had been in command of 1st Northamptonshire Battery since May 1910. The Foot family's connection with the brigade was not yet lost, however, for Colonel Foot's only son, R.C. Foot had been commissioned in 2nd Herts Battery in March 1912. As the brigade's first commanding officer, Colonel Foot had played a key role in shaping the peace-time organisation and the recruiting areas of the batteries, and in the eventual raising of the brigade ammunition column. Above all, though, he had set, at an early stage, high standards of preparation and training for the limited war then foreseen for the Territorials, that were to be tested all too soon.

PLATE II   An evening drill at St. Albans, c.1912
(From the water-colour specially painted for this work by Joan Wanklyn, 1996)

Between 1908 and 1914 both 1st and 2nd Hertfordshire Batteries held evening drill parades, sometimes more than twice a week, in the three months or so preceding annual camp, which usually took place during the first two weeks of August. Notice of parades was given in the local press and mounted drills took place on open ground conveniently close to the battery drill halls. Here, 1st Hertfordshire Battery have fielded a gun with 6-horse team and one ammunition wagon with 4-horse team. Earlier in the day the necessary horses would have been reclaimed from the farms and businesses where they were boarded out and they would, of course, have had to be returned after training had finished.

Chapter 4

At War – Approach March, Action and Stalemate

Mobilisation and Service at War Stations, August 1914–November 1915

Lieutenant-Colonel Lord Exeter had taken command of a usefully recruited brigade with high standards of training and was no doubt looking forward to his first camp in command as the four brigades of the East Anglian Divisional Artillery converged on the Redesdale training area in Northumberland at the beginning of August 1914. As things turned out, he was to spend rather more than fifteen days in full-time command, for only a few hours after the main body of 4th East Anglian Brigade had arrived on 3rd August – the men were sitting down to their evening meal at about 6.00 p.m. – a telegram was received ordering all units to return to their home stations at once. Mobilisation was clearly imminent, and embodiment of the Territorial Force was proclaimed on 4th August; the actual order to mobilise arrived at drill halls at about 5.00 p.m. Redesdale Camp was some two miles from the nearest railway station, which was on a single-track branch line. With remarkable understatement, F.E.C. Stanley, who was about to be promoted captain in 1st Northants Battery, and whose *Short History of the Northamptonshire Battery* is an important source, recorded:

> ". . . the necessary trains to move the Divisional Artillery took time to assemble. Major Walker, with about half the battery, got away at 9.00 p.m. on the 5th; and Lieutenants Stanley and Phillips followed with the remainder soon after dawn the next morning, arriving at Peterborough at about 1.45 p.m. on 6th August.
>
> Major Walker, on arrival, commandeered the whole of the accommodation at Messrs. Sexton's repository and arranged for the rank and file to mess at the Bedford Coffee House. Horses were stabled in the loose boxes and guards mounted at the repository and drill hall gates.
>
> The battery commander met the second train at 1.45 p.m. The newly arrived men were marched off to dinner, horses and vehicles being taken to stables and gun park by a party from the first train. After stables and guard mounting, the men were dismissed to their homes for the night, with orders to parade at 6.00 a.m. next day. A few who lived outside the city were accommodated in the drill hall and Lieutenants Stanley and Phillips were billeted at the Angel Hotel."

Similar scenes were, of course, enacted at St. Albans and Watford.

The mobilisation timetable allowed four days for Territorial Force units to reorganise to war establishment, draw or requisition horses, wagons and other material not held in peace-time, and report ready to move to war stations. The plan did not specify how units were to reach war establishment in men but in 4th East Anglian Brigade's case large numbers of former members applied to rejoin and there was no shortage of new recruits, who would be trained by batteries at their war stations. Little detail survives of these first, hectic days of war. It is evident that the Hertfordshire batteries completed the process of mobilisation rather earlier that the Peterborough battery, though there is room for doubt whether things went quite as smoothly as subsequently reported by Griffith (see Bibliography) – ". . . on the fourth day of mobilisation, 8th August, exactly in accordance with their mobilisation timetable, they marched by road to their war stations in Essex, complete to the last button, strap and nut". The Hertfordshire batteries were within road-march distance of their concentration area, which was centred on the East Anglian Division's peace-time headquarters at Warley, near [39]

Plate 33   *2nd Hertfordshire Battery mobilise
and move to war stations, Watford, August 1914.*
Top – *An off-duty group at Clarendon Hall*
(above). *The scene at Clarendon Hall as the
battery prepared to move* (below).
Bottom – *The column forming up in Clarendon
Road* (above) *and moving through High Street*
(below).

(Watford Library)   [40]

Brentwood. The Peterborough battery had a great deal further to travel and went by train to Ongar, arriving during Sunday, 12th August. On 20th August the East Anglian Division deployed to counter-invasion stations which were some distance from the coast – divisional headquarters was at Bury St. Edmunds and the 'line' stretched north to Norwich and south to Chelmsford. The 4th East Anglian Brigade was allocated an area around Euston, near Thetford and moved into billets in substantial country houses, where there was room for the horses, guns and wagons, as well as officers and men. Once established in their new locations, the batteries were paraded and all ranks were invited to volunteer for 'Imperial Service', i.e., service abroad, either with the Expeditionary Force in France or in one of Britain's many overseas garrisons. There is no record of the exact numbers who volunteered but they were sufficient for all three batteries to be designated Imperial Service units. The brigade ammunition column was not accepted until early October, probably because of the number of untrained recruits, rather than lack of volunteers for service abroad. 'Reserve' batteries were formed with effect from 1st September 1914, each around a nucleus of former members of the original batteries who either had not volunteered for foreign service or who were above the age limits or in some way unfit for active serve abroad (see page 6). By mid-September the original or '1st Line' batteries of 4th East Anglian Brigade were up to establishment in non-commissioned officers and men and the brigade ammunition column was only a handful of men short. Some half-dozen officers were still required for the brigade as a whole.

During September 1914 there were several invasion scares and Stanley records that on one occasion the brigade was called out to battle positions in the East Coast Defences and had actually moved several miles before confirmation of a false alarm was received. Similarly, as the winter of 1914–15 progressed, the brigade was more than once placed on 'instant readiness' but the 'stand down' message sent officers and men back to whichever activity had been

Plate 34   *The Battery Sergeant-Major and Senior Non-Commissioned Officers of 2nd Hertfordshire Battery, October 1914. Standing (L.–R.) Sgt. Seabrook, Fitter-Sgt. Jones, Saddler-Sgt. Jones, Sgt. Wingfield, Sgt. Hurcomb; Seated (L.–R.) Sgt. Humphries, B.Q.M.S. Smith, B.S.M. Coles, Farrier-Sgt. Butcher, Sgt. Hancock.*   (Watford Library)

Plate 35   *2nd Hertfordshire Battery in camp near Kings Langley, July 1915.*
Top – *The gun park on the common* (above); *cookhouse fatigues* (below).
Bottom – *The battery cooks at work* (above); *the mid-day meal* (below).   (Watford Library)   [42]

Plate 36 *Riding horses of 2nd Herts Battery at Kings Langley, July 1915.* (Watford Library)

interrupted. In any horsed unit there was always plenty to do to maintain the animals in a healthy, active condition – a necessary prerequisite to their use in training, or eventually in battle. Stanley recalls "intensive training in every branch of the work", while E.J.T. Lutyens, who joined 1st Herts Battery on commissioning in November 1914, recorded in a later memoir (see Bibliography) that his main impression was of "driving drills in Euston Park, all-night diggings-in and horse parades". The average age of the horses, according to Lutyens, was about 25 years and "the chief hobby of inspecting generals seemed to be to parade these antiques in a north-east wind, and when they had them frozen to the bone to pinch them and call them 'hide-bound'". Invasion scares and over-age horses were not the only thing that stuck in the mind. Many years later, Lord Oaksey, then Lieutenant Geoffrey Lawrence, referred to the increasing number of German Zeppelin airships attempting to cross the coast with the eventual intention of bombing targets in or near London. Orders were received that, on identifying Zeppelins, batteries were to engage them "with gun and rifle fire". Pits were accordingly dug, into which the trails were lowered to achieve the necessary elevation of the gun barrels. It is not recorded whether any tables were issued for the calculation of height of burst of shrapnel shell but it is probably fortunate that this primitive form of anti-aircraft defence was never put to the test of live firing.

In April 1915 the brigade, now designated 1st/4th East Anglian Brigade to denote its Imperial Service status (see page 6), went to practice camp on Salisbury Plain. It returned to Euston to find that the East Anglian Division, which was designated 54th (East Anglian) Division early in May 1915, had been ordered to leave its coast defence positions and concentrate in and near St. Albans, evidently to await detailed orders for service abroad. An area around Hemel Hempstead was allocated to 1st/4th East Anglian Brigade, so by a happy chance, the Hertfordshire batteries were back in their own county, with 1st/2nd Herts Battery [43]

Plate 37 *2nd Herts Battery march away from Kings Langley – the head of the column in Market Place, Watford, July 1915.* (Watford Library)

actually in the middle of their own recruiting area. The other two county units, 1st/1st Hertfordshire Yeomanry and 1st/1st Battalion The Hertfordshire Regiment, had both left for service abroad some months before, so local newspapers were able, as far as the relatively primitive security measures then in force permitted, to cover fully the return to the county of its only 1st Line unit still in Britain. The *Watford Illustrated*, which had been founded at the outbreak of war specifically to provide a weekly illustrated record of events affecting the district, was particularly generous in its coverage.

On 8th July 1915, some eight weeks after reaching St. Albans, 54th Division was ordered to prepare to move to the Dardanelles. Conditions on the Gallipoli peninsula were so difficult, largely through overcrowding of the beach-heads, that the whole of the divisional artillery and the greater part of the divisional train had to remain in England. This news came as a disappointment to all those left behind as the division moved to its embarkation ports between 20th–30th July, and after another week in Hertfordshire the divisional artillery marched back to the Thetford area of Norfolk and was attached to 69th (2nd East Anglian) Divisional Artillery – an arrangement which at least gave 1st/4th East Anglian Brigade the opportunity of closer contact with their affiliated 2nd Line brigade – 2nd/4th East Anglian Brigade.

It was to be more than three months before the 54th Divisional Artillery could be found useful employment. Meanwhile, commanders at all levels struggled to think of ways of providing "interesting and useful variation in the monotony of continual training of all ranks who had long been in the highest possible condition of fitness for anything they might be called upon to do, and were losing heart at the long delay in getting abroad" (Stanley). One of the C.R.A.'s contributions, during September, was an 'Emergency Move Competition'. No details of the competition itself have survived but evidently one battery represented each brigade and in 1st/4th East Anglian Brigade's case it was 1st/1st Herts Battery. The battery orders book (now in the Regimental Collection) records in detail the battery's 'order of battle' for the event, in which 101 officers and men and 106 horses took part. Each of the four sub-sections fielded its full war establishment of gun and two first-line ammunition wagons, all with six-horse teams, and it is only the inclusion of the names of all the horses that makes the 1915 order of battle substantially different from one that might be published by 1st/1st Herts Battery's present-day successors. The names of C Sub-Section's gun team have a particular appeal – Lead: Beauty and Bennice; Centre: Jeannie and Sam; Wheel: Mabel and Madge – and other well matched pairs included Ginger and Pop and Oxford and Cambridge. (A vehicle 'tac sign' or registration number just does not have the same ring!)

The weeks spent in the Hertfordshire batteries' home ground were perhaps in Major Tom Walker's mind when he suggested that 1st/1st Northants Battery should carry out a march through their recruiting area, visiting, and staying in, the principal towns, including Peterborough, Oundle, Kettering, Stamford and Huntingdon. The march, which took place during October, was, according to Stanley, "entirely successful and enjoyable". Not only did it 'beat the drum' and draw attention to the need for recruits, for the battery and for other county units as well, but it enabled the men to see something of their relatives and friends. Like the stay at Hemel Hempstead, the march was well covered by the local press and quite a number of photographs were taken.

A Few Shots in Anger – France, November 1915–January 1916

Soon after the Peterborough battery's return to Thetford, 1st/4th East Anglian Brigade, in common with all other units of the 54th Divisional Artillery, received orders to prepare for service abroad. At almost the last moment, the 15-pdr. B.L.C. guns and their associated ammunition wagons were handed over to 69th Divisional Artillery, who up to this time had had only a few antique French 90-mm. guns for training, and the batteries were issued with new 18-pdr. guns and wagons – but still only to the Territorial Force war establishment of four guns to a battery. On 16th November 1915 the brigade entrained at Thetford for the journey to Southampton, where they embarked for Le Havre, sailing on the night of 17th November. The decision to send 54th Divisional Artillery to France, perhaps originally made on the grounds that the additional firepower would be welcome and the troops would gain valuable experience, now seems questionable, for their parent division began its withdrawal from the Gallipoli peninsula only a week later.

In his *The Forgotten Fronts . . .*, Sir Martin Farndale (see Bibliography) states that 54th

Plate 38 *Major T.H. Walker, followed by Trumpeter Lambert and B.S.M. Stimpson, leading 1st/1st Northamptonshire Battery along Newark Hill, Peterborough during the march through the battery's recruiting area, October 1915.* (Peterborough Museum)

Divisional Artillery had "considerable active experience in the battles in France" but, at least as far as 1st/4th East Anglian Brigade was concerned, this does not seem to be true, certainly not from the point of view of the 'gun end'. The brigade moved by rail from Le Havre to St. Omer and then marched to billets in villages near Béthune. For the next five weeks, until immediately before Christmas, parties of officers and signallers were attached for periods of a few days to the observation posts of batteries which had been in action in the area for some time and could pass on to the newcomers "the intricacies of that particular part of the front and the special methods employed there." Stanley's account continues:

"This kind of work went on until Christmas, which was spent in the village of Lières not far from Béthune. Almost directly after, orders were received for the batteries to go into the line, and dates were fixed for them to take over certain positions in action. A Battery (*1st/1st Herts*) was the first to move and marched out one morning. It got into action, and had scarcely settled down when it was ordered out again and sent back to Lières, which it reached very late the same night. Then it was learned that the whole plan had been altered."

The battery had spent an active day firing from a position in the grounds of the chateau at Vermelles and returned to billets to find four different rumours about their eventual destination were circulating – Italy, Salonika, Egypt or Mesopotamia. It was to be nearly a month before their destination was known and meanwhile, for reasons which are not on record, the brigade was split in two. Each battery was to leave behind all its drivers, horses and ammunition wagons, under command of the battery captain, while remaining personnel and the guns went by train to Marseilles. Stanley, battery captain of 1st/1st Northants Battery, records that there followed "three weeks' comfortable residence in a brewery", while Lutyens, who went to Marseilles with 1st/1st Herts Battery's guns, later described "a glorious three weeks in the sun, during which, as signallers, some of us climbed the wooded mountain sides to helio from peak to peak". If there was ever a plan to retain the wagons in France, perhaps as the basis for a divisional ammunition column, somebody, fortunately, thought better of it and the complete brigade reassembled at La Valentine, outside Marseilles and received orders to proceed to Egypt and rejoin 54th Division.

The batteries and the ammunition column were split between three ships, the transports *Andania*, *Rhesus* and *Missouri*. They embarked on 3rd February 1916 and sailed the following day. Aboard *Rhesus*, in response to a warning that enemy submarines were active, four guns were brought on deck and the wheels mounted on sandbags so that the trails could be dropped a little, to increase the possible range to five thousand yards. As with the earlier anti-Zeppelin arrangements, these primitive anti-submarine measures were not put to the test, for, as the brigade war diary recorded, "No target presented itself". The voyage appears to have been considerably helped by fine weather and good sea conditions, for Lutyens recalled that, [45]

Plate 39 *A smartly turned-out ammunition wagon in Peterborough during the march, October 1915. Note the breast-collar draught harness, which replaced neck-collar harness (Plate 29) after mobilisation.* (Regimental Collection)

also aboard *Rhesus*, they had managed to get each of the 120 horses on deck for exercise every day throughout the six-day voyage. It is clear that no attempt had been made at what is today described as 'combat loading' of the three ships. Indeed it is possible that they were loaded according to the two groups into which the brigade had been divided a month earlier. Lutyens recorded:

> "On 8th February we arrived at Alexandria and went straight on to Cairo, arriving in the early hours of the morning. The drivers were on a different boat, and so it happened that the gunners were faced with sacks of harness of which they had a somewhat scanty knowledge. However, we managed to harness up and get away in a very short space of time, and began to march through Cairo towards Mena."

The 54th Division had been at Mena Camp, quite close to the pyramids, since before Christmas, resting and refitting after the campaign in Gallipoli. The division would shortly join the reorganised defences of the Suez Canal. Meanwhile 1st/4th East Anglian Brigade resumed training in the new, desert conditions, the batteries going out every day "doing drill orders on the desert and driving drill on the hard, flat bits of sand, chiefly round the pyramids" (Lutyens). Practice firing took place in the desert in the middle of March, by which time the units of the divisional artillery were ready to take their place alongside the now battle-experienced infantry battalions of the division.

Suez Canal Defences – Egypt, February 1916–January 1917

The Turks had made one attempt to cross the Suez Canal in February 1915, as a result of which steps were taken to improve considerably its defences. The new plan, which was implemented late in 1915, relied on dominating the eastern bank for a distance of seven miles, thus ensuring that the Turks were kept beyond artillery range of the Canal itself. A line of strong points was established in the desert, many of them connected with the canal bank by light railway. The strong points and satellite trench systems were continuously manned by infantry, usually in at least company strength, and the area for several miles in front was frequently patrolled by infantry, mounted and camel troops, in order to deny the enemy the use of the wells and cisterns to be found at intervals in the desert. During the first few days of April 1916, 54th Division moved to take over part of the Suez Canal defences. The division released 163 Infantry Brigade to come under command of the neighbouring 53rd Division but was reinforced by the addition of two Indian infantry brigades and took over No. 1 Section, which stretched from Ayun Musa, on the eastern shore of the Red Sea, south-east of Suez, northwards to a point about half way up the Great Bitter Lake.

On 29th March 1916, advance parties left Mena Camp for El Kubri and Shallufa, points on the Canal between Suez and the Great Bitter Lake from both of which light railways extended eastward into the desert to defended localities. Second Lieutenant Lutyens with Right Section, 1st/1st Herts Battery, moved out almost at once some seven miles into the desert from Shallufa to a strong point known as Wigan Post. He recorded no detail of artillery tactics and [46] technicalities but noted, "We thoroughly enjoyed our stay there, chiefly owing to a case of

Plate 40   *Major Geoffrey Lawrence, who rose from Second Lieutenant to Major, Commanding 1st/1st Hertfordshire Battery in the first seven months of the war and commanded the battery throughout the campaign in Egypt and Palestine. He was mentioned in despatches for services at the Second Battle of Gaza and appointed to the Distinguished Service Order later in the campaign.* (Regimental Collection)

scarlet fever, which kept all the staff away". The garrison of Wigan Post held a sports meeting at Easter, with mounted and foot races, football, wrestling on horseback and a steeplechase for the 'Wigan Hunt Cup'. The summer heat dictated the day's timetable – "From 10.00 a.m. to 3.00 p.m. no one was allowed out of his bivvy, where he lay on his ground-sheet in his birth-day suit, while the sweat formed in little pools under him. Then it would get cooler and we could proceed with the days work".

The cumbersome titles of Territorial artillery brigades and batteries were not addressed in 54th Division until the end of May 1916, and, curiously, not all on the same day. Under the new system, which used Roman numerals, 1st/4th East Anglian Brigade, R.F.A. became CCLXXIII Brigade, R.F.A., known generally as 273 Brigade. The batteries were lettered according to their seniority within the brigade, 1st/1st Herts Battery becoming A Battery (A/273), 1st/2nd Herts Battery, B Battery (B/273) and 1st/1st Northants Battery, C Battery (C/273), [47]

Plate 41   *Off duty during the early weeks in Egypt, February–March 1916. Three sergeants of 1st/1st Herts Battery in Cairo wearing newly-issued khaki drill tunics and shorts.* (Regimental Collection)

with no change in their four-gun establishment and organisation. On the same day, 29th May, 273 Brigade moved from its dispersed positions around Shallufa and El Kubri to Serapeum, immediately to the north of the Great Bitter Lake and in 53rd Division's No. 1 Section. The reason for this move is not explained in the *Official History*, *Despatches* or any unit records but 163 Infantry Brigade of 54th Division is shown in the *Official History* (Vol. I, Map 7) as being under command of 53rd Division in July 1916, and in all probability 273 Brigade was placed under command as well, as the supporting artillery brigade.

Captain Stanley's description of life at Serapeum Railhead is, like Lutyens' record of Wigan Post, short of detail on artillery matters. It was by now well into the Egyptian summer, which was evidently less appealing to C Battery:

"This was the battery's first experience of real, unadulterated desert. There was not a sign of anything but sand all round. Here was spent the hottest summer recorded for thirty-five years. In a temperature of 120 degrees in the shade during many weeks, the battery was occupied fortifying the range of low hills and sand dunes to the east for the protection of the Canal against the renewed attack by the Turks, which was daily expected but never came off.

The heat, the flies, and the large amount of work that had to be done, combined to make it a time to try the toughest, and fortunate was the officer or man who escaped sceptic sores for any length of time. Nearly everyone had a bandage on leg, arm or hand. One of the gunners, in a letter home, described the life during these long months in words that deserve permanent record – 'Dear . . ., This war is a fair beggar. There is nothing but sand here. Half of it we eat, and the rest we put into bags'."

Second Lieutenant Lutyens was at the very same place, though it would be hard to guess as much from his description:

"In June the battery joined up again and we moved to Serapeum Railhead, where we remained until Christmas. I think that this was the best part of the war for us. The climate was ideal, and we had every kind of game – cricket in the sand on matting wickets, rugger against several teams . . . soccer, bathing parties on horseback down to the Canal – not to forget drill orders on the sand, and horse coping galore. By this time, under Major Lawrence's careful selection, we had undoubtedly the finest lot of horses of any battery in Egypt, and the drivers were now as good as a Regular battery at horse management and driving, all of which was shortly going to be put to a very serious test."

Immediately before the move to Serapeum, Captain V.H. Bailey, who had left Oxford to follow his brother, E.A.H. Bailey, into 2nd Herts Battery on the outbreak of war, was appointed adjutant. The new adjutant was a meticulous diarist, able to observe from a key position, and left a most valuable record of the brigade's activities until he was posted out in May 1918. On 11th December 1916 he noted:

Plate 42   *Men of 1st/1st Herts Battery taking a break between duties at Serapeum Railhead, 1916. Infantry parading in the background emphasise the 'all arms' nature of the force at Serapeum.*

(Regimental Collection)

Plate 43   *Transport of 273 Brigade in Egypt, 1916. Left – Limbered general service wagons, probably of the brigade ammunition column but evidently being used to transport 'miscellaneous stores'. Right – An ammunition wagon in difficulty while crossing the Sweet Water Canal.*   (Regimental Collection)

"Orders came in about composite field artillery brigades – two 6-gun 18-pdr. and one 4-gun 4.5-in. howitzer battery per brigade. It will mean making our three 4-gun 18-pdr. batteries into two 6-gun batteries."

Two days later there was a conference of battery commanders to discuss the splitting up of B Battery (formerly 1st/2nd Herts Battery), so it had evidently been decided, not unreasonably, that the link with Hertfordshire should be maintained by one of the new 18-pdr. batteries and the link with Northamptonshire by the other. On 18th December the reorganisation took place, with the note "All horses, guns and equipment of B taken over by A and C". The East Anglian Divisional Artillery's 2-battery howitzer brigade was raised in Suffolk, as 3rd East Anglian (Howitzer) Brigade, with 1st and 2nd Suffolk (Howitzer) Batteries. On 28th May 1916, 1st/3rd East Anglian (Howitzer) Brigade had been redesignated CCLXXII (272) Brigade and its batteries lettered A and B. Now the original 1st/2nd Suffolk (Howitzer) Battery (B/272) joined the Herts and Northants batteries on 21st December 1916 in the new-style field artillery brigade, which was then designated CCLXX (270) Brigade. It was, accordingly, as 270 Brigade with A/270 (Herts), B/270 (Northants) and C/270(How.) (Suffolk) that the officers and men of the St. Albans, Watford and Peterborough batteries were to see action in the battles on the north-eastern frontier of Egypt and in the advance through Palestine that would follow in 1917 and 1918.

More than two years of waiting was about to end but before they reached the front, 270 Brigade had to contend with yet another upheaval, the impact of which is unfortunately not recorded in Captain Bailey's diary. The changes in the administration of the Territorial artillery by the County Associations at home are described briefly in Chapter 1. It is not clear how long it took for news of these changes, and instructions on their implementation, to reach 270 Brigade, who probably felt that they had had enough change for the time being, anyway. Under A.C.I. 2185, issued on 20th November 1916, Hertfordshire Association became responsible for the administration of soldiers recruited in Northamptonshire. The association was allocated the block of numbers 890001–895000 under the renumbering scheme introduced by A.C.I. 2198 of 1916 and evidently decided that there was advantage in being able to identify the county in which a soldier had enlisted by his number. Hertfordshire men were accordingly given numbers starting with 890001, while those from Northamptonshire were numbered [49]

Plate 44 *Close order driving drill, A Battery, 273 Brigade, Egypt, 1916.* (Regimental Collection)

from 891001. It is not known whether other associations adopted the same method of distinguishing between their counties but it is fortunate that Hertfordshire did so, for it is unusual for lists, e.g., of casualties or recipients of decorations, to distinguish between batteries. The third county represented in 270 Brigade – Suffolk – was allocated 885001–890000 for their howitzer batteries. Suffolk also administered the divisional ammunition column, soldiers from which were sometimes transferred into 270 Brigade. They are recognisable by their numbers beginning with 895001. The implementation date for the renumbering scheme was twice put off, to an eventual date of 15th February 1917, by which time 270 Brigade was well on the way across the Sinai desert.

War in Earnest – The First and Second Battles of Gaza, February–April 1917

While the 54th Division went about the unglamorous but essential duty of defending the Suez Canal, gradual progress was made in pushing the Turks back along the Mediterranean coast. The battle of Romani, early in August 1916, opened the way for the advance towards El Arish and the Egypt–Palestine frontier at Rafa, but the pace of the advance was slowed by the need to supply the troops with water, for which a pipeline was constructed, and all forms of stores, which were brought forward by rail, again on a line laid for the purpose. El Arish was abandoned by the Turks on 21st December 1916 and at once occupied. Actions followed at Magdhaba, on 23rd December, and at Rafa on 9th January 1917, after which Eastern Force stood on the frontier ready to probe north-eastwards towards the first major objective in Palestine – the city of Gaza. Ordered to send the 42nd Division to France, and warned that the reinforcements he judged necessary for an advance into Palestine could not be sent, General Murray nevertheless prepared to continue, and withdrew the 54th Division from the Canal Defences to join Eastern Force.

Between 8th and 10th January 1917, the batteries and ammunition column of 270 Brigade left their positions on the Canal to concentrate with the rest of 54th Division at Moascar, near Ismailia. Here Lieutenant-Colonel Lord Exeter had, for the first time, the whole of his new command in one place, and the new A and B Batteries (Major Geoffrey Lawrence and Major F.E.C. Stanley) were able to make contact with C(Howitzer) Battery (Major W. J. von Pendlebury). The last two weeks of January were spent in refitting and training with the affiliated infantry brigade. The trek towards the battle front began on 1st February and at the end of the second day's march 270 Brigade reached Kantara. Here, as part of a plan to

[50]

Plate 45 *270 Brigade's trek across the Sinai Desert towards Gaza, February–March 1917.*
Top – *A Battery column moving away from Moascar on 1st February.*
Bottom – *B Sub-Section of A Battery halted in the desert. Note the ped-rails on the wheels and the twelve-horse team, with drivers on the outside horses of each group of four.*
(Regimental Collection)

release wheeled transport, which was in short supply, for the formations due to follow up after the capture of Gaza, and to allow for 12-horse teams for guns and ammunition wagons, the brigade was reorganised to camel transport establishment. Stanley records that in B Battery:

"The simple comforts that had been collected in the desert – luxuries like tents and camp beds, and the almost indispensable mess cart and water cart – were taken away and seventeen camels were provided to carry everything that could not reasonably be taken on the ammunition wagons or saddles. The wagons were more than loaded with men's blankets, farriers', fitters' and saddlers' tools, spare signalling gear and so on; officers' valises were down to the barest limits and the men had only their haversacks. When at last the battery got away from Kantara (*it was*) past the eyes of as many generals as could find an excuse to come and say 'you have got far too much on your vehicles', without hinting at any other means of carrying what few posessions remained . . ."

The brigade war diary records a much more significant effect of the reduction to camel transport establishment – no sooner had the 18-pdr. batteries been increased to six guns, than they were ordered to select two guns each to be 'left out of battle' with one officer and their detachments, so that the horses thus released could be included in the double-teams. The brigade ammunition column, too, was reduced to two 'depot sections', which were concentrated with the depot sections of the other brigades of the divisional artillery – a forerunner of the eventual divisional ammunition column. There were no roads forward of Kantara and 'ped-rails' – blocks of wood some 24 inches x 10 inches were fixed round the wheels of guns and wagons, giving greatly reduced ground pressure compared with the iron tyres, and considerably easing progress across the soft sand, into which the horses' hooves sometimes sank more than twelve inches.

[51]

Plate 46 *The trek to the front at Gaza, as experienced by A Battery, 270 Brigade, February 1917.*
Top – *Horse lines under palm trees at Romani.*
Centre – *Camels resting during a halt in the desert.*
Bottom – *A Sub-Section at work on the defences of El Arish.*
(Regimental Collection) [52]

Plate 47 *Scenes at Deir el Belah as A/270 waited to move forward to the Gaza front, March 1917.*
Top – *The battery wagon lines. Note the deep hoof prints in the soft sand (foreground).*
Centre – *Horse lines. Ped-rails have been removed from the limber (left) and ammunition wagon (right) but one set can be seen on the ground.*
Bottom – *Camel lines.*
(Regimental Collection)

[53]

The greater part of the approach march – some one hundred miles out of the total of about one hundred and forty from Kantara to the divisional concentration area at In Seirat – had been completed when the brigade reached El Arish on 25th February. Three days earlier news had reached 270 Brigade that Lieutenant-Colonel Lord Exeter was to transfer to command of the Royal Horse Artillery of the Imperial Mounted Division and would be succeeded in command of the brigade by Lieutenant-Colonel H. Sowler, transferred from 42nd Divisional Artillery. The march was interrupted for two weeks at El Arish, where officers and men worked on the ever-expanding defences, and for a further twelve days at El Burj, where 270 Brigade joined up with 162 Infantry Brigade, which they would be supporting in action. From 20th March onwards a series of carefully controlled moves, usually by night, brought the whole of the attacking force forward to concentration areas some eight to ten miles south-west of Gaza.

Orders for an attack on Gaza, later known as the First Battle of Gaza, were issued by Headquarters Eastern Force on 24th March 1917. They laid down that the operation should begin on 26th March and separated the formations involved into Desert Column (two mounted divisions and 53rd Infantry Division), which would undertake the attack on Gaza itself, and those retained under direct command of G.O.C. Eastern Force (the Imperial Camel Brigade, 52nd and 54th Infantry Divisions and 229 Infantry Brigade). The two mounted divisions of Desert Column were to make a wide right-flanking movement to cut off the Turks' retreat from Gaza, while 53rd Division advanced against the city from the south. The 54th Division was to move out to the Sheikh Abbas ridge, some five miles south-south-east of Gaza and there take up a position protecting the right flank of Desert Column against Turkish counter-attack from the east.

A necessary preliminary to the attack on Gaza was the crossing of the Wadi Guzze, an almost dry water course about one hundred yards across and 45 feet deep, which ran northwards to reach the sea about five miles south of Gaza and formed a natural barrier to the progress of Eastern Force. Extensive reconnaissance up to, but not beyond, the Wadi Guzze took place on 25th March. Then, early in the morning of 26th March, under cover of a dense sea fog, the two mounted divisions crossed the wadi and began their encirclement of Gaza. Immediately behind these formations, 54th Divisional Cavalry Squadron (A Squadron, 1st/1st Hertfordshire Yeomanry) crossed as the leading element of the division, with orders to occupy the Sheikh Abbas ridge and hold it until relieved by the leading infantry – 163 Brigade – who arrived about noon and began to dig in facing east. Shortly afterwards 162 Brigade took up a position on high ground further along the ridge to the south-west and an outpost line was established across the whole of the divisional front. (The division was operating with only two infantry brigades and one artillery brigade – 270 – having left one artillery brigade in the Canal Defences and had one infantry brigade and one artillery brigade detached to Eastern Force reserve). It proved more difficult than expected to get the guns and wagons of 270 Brigade across the Wadi Guzze and it was early afternoon before they moved into action on the ridge and deployed forward observation officers with the outposts to take advantage of the "commanding view of the low country to the east – a green sea of barley stretching far in the direction of Beersheba" (Stanley). The expected Turkish counter-attack, which "would have presented magnificent targets to us" failed to materialise and:

"Towards sunset we consumed the remains of such food as we carried and prepared to set-tle down for the night, hoping our ration camels might somehow find us before morning. However, just as the last gleam of day disappeared, orders arrived for us to move at once. So, with horses still unwatered and rations still somewhere in the blue, we hooked in our weary teams once more and started off into the unknown, in the direction of Gaza.

The route took us over the worst possible ground – very broken and hard, and serrated with wadis big and little. The further we went, the more awful became the going; there was no moon and we had no idea where we were or what was in front of us. Almost every few yards there was a check and vehicles had constantly to be manhandled out of bad places . . . How far in miles we travelled that night I never discovered. It could not have been more than four . . . Thoroughly tired out, we somehow got the horses picketed and it was nearly 2.00 a.m. on the 27th when, at length, I found a couple of blankets . . . and lay down.

PLATE III   Advancing towards Gaza, 26th March 1917
(From the water-colour specially painted for this work by Joan Wanklyn, 1996)

The appalling 'going' as the batteries of 270 Brigade approached the Gaza battlefield – areas of deep sand with steep-sided wadis at intervals – was overcome by the use of 'ped-rails', which greatly reduced the ground pressure of the narrow, iron-tyred wheels, and double teams on guns and ammunition wagons. Based on a photograph taken as the guns of A/270 approached their first position on the Sheikh Abbas ridge, this painting shows an 18-pdr. gun negotiating a difficult wadi, the bed of which has already been 'improved' by a working party. No extra horses were available and even after camels and mules had been added to the establishment in substitution for horses, there were still not enough horses to provide double teams for all six guns and their ammunition wagons, with the result that the 18-pdr. batteries took only four of their six guns into action.

Plate 48   *The First Battle of Gaza, March 1917.*
Top – *18-pdrs. of A/270, pulled by 12-horse teams, crossing a wadi during the approach to the first gun position* (see also Coloured Plate III).
Bottom – *A Battery seize the opportunity to water some of their horses at the well at Sharta.*
(Regimental Collection)

By a stroke of genius, B.Q.M.S. Griffin had found us during the night. He had got all his camels up without a casualty, and, as I walked round the bivouac (*at 4.00 a.m.*), I found the cooks already busy with breakfast and the horses being fed. Water for them, however, was out of the question . . . About 5.00 a.m. we saddled up and the brigade moved off, roughly east . . . After going a very short distance, with many checks, we were formed up to await further orders . . . (*Now that it was daylight*) all that we could see was that we were on fairly flat ground . . . falling away to the south towards the Wadi Guzze, far below us and three miles distant."

Stanley goes on to say that he was able to discover that Gaza was now some three miles away to the north but that it was not even clear whether it had been captured or was still in Turkish hands. ("News was of the very vaguest . . . and what was going to happen seemed impossible to discover.") In fact, the encircling movement by the mounted troops of Desert Column had been entirely successful but the attack by 53rd Division had started late. Nevertheless, patrols from the cavalry to the north and 53rd Division to the south actually met in Gaza as darkness fell. By now, however, following reports of enemy reinforcements moving towards Gaza from the east, and taking into account the fact that most of the mounted troops had not been able to water their horses all day, General Dobell, commanding Eastern Force, ordered that unless Gaza itself had been captured before nightfall, the mounted divisions should be withdrawn to the Wadi Guzze. To the forward troops on the ground, it seemed as if 'defeat had been snatched from the jaws of victory', but the causes of failure were complex (see *Official History* and Bullock, whose brief comments include the expression "staff farce"). There were faults in organisation, command and control, and battlefield communications and, by later standards, there was a noticeable shortage of artillery.

B Battery's difficult night, described above, resulted from the decision to withdraw 53rd Division from its footholds in Gaza, and 54th Division from the Sheikh Abbas ridge, to mutu- [55]

ally supporting positions south of Gaza. These moves proved too difficult to carry out in the dark and at dawn the divisions found themselves back-to-back in a salient, based on the Wadi Guzze and stretching north-eastwards to include the high ground at Ali Muntar, overlooking Gaza and the Beersheba road. Turkish counter-attacks began in earnest at about 9.30 a.m. on 27th March. Ali Muntar was quickly recaptured and the tip of the British salient pushed to the south-west. It was by now recognised that any chance of re-establishing the positions of the previous evening and completing the capture of Gaza had slipped away and that withdrawal across the Wadi Guzze was the only option. Orders to that effect were given at 4.30 p.m. Meanwhile, 270 Brigade were in action all day from positions on the Mansura ridge, dealing not only with Turkish infantry advancing across the Sheikh Abbas ridge to the east, but having to 'switch' more than ninety degrees to help break up counter-attacks launched from Gaza itself, and undertake 'counter-battery' tasks when Turkish field guns were observed in action against the supported infantry or the batteries of the brigade. The "most dramatic target of all" (Griffith) was a troop of Turkish cavalry "who were unlucky enough to walk slowly, in close order, over a piece of ground that B Battery had just registered . . . Under the sudden squall of shrapnel that beat down upon them, men and horses simply ceased to exist". But the casualties on this, the batteries' first day of real fighting since the war began, were not all on the Turkish side. A Battery was caught in enfilade at one point and the wagon lines were frequently forced to move. Stanley recorded:

> "I heard afterwards that B Battery had caught it pretty well as they came into action, that Longmore had coolly worked out the lines for the guns in a shower of shrapnel, but mercifully was untouched, and that gun shields and wagon bodies had been well splashed with bullets, while several men had pieces taken out of caps or sleeves. Sergeant Barker, however, had been the only man really hit. He had been very severely wounded in the right arm and side but gallantly refused to be taken away from his gun and lay on the ground directing its service for some time. His strength gave out at last and he was carried off to hospital, whence he did not return for several months . . . He eventually received the Distinguished Conduct Medal."

Darkness fell at about 6.00 p.m., after which 270 Brigade took no further part in the battle. In contrast to the first day, the second had been one of furious activity and very hard work both for the gun detachments, who had to contend with frequent large switches and the hot, dry 'khamseen', which blew all day, and for the ammunition wagons, for the nearest dump was some three miles away in the Wadi Guzze and the teams had to do several rough journeys each, all at best possible speed. Only a very few of the horses were watered on their journeys to the ammunition dump and by nightfall on 27th March the majority had not drunk for 48 hours.

Well into the evening orders came to withdraw to the area of Deir el Belah and "Sad and miserably weary, hungry, thirsty and cold, we mounted and trekked away into the night, hoping that someone in front knew the way and expecting to be attacked at any moment from the flank" (Stanley). The brigade was down to its last spare wagon pole. Many had broken under the rough going after months drying out in the sun, and the journey was punctuated by unscheduled halts at which it became commonplace to see men fall from their horses and sleep where fell. There was little time for real rest, even after the batteries reached their bivouac area between 4.00 and 6.00 a.m. on 28th March. The Wadi Guzze now became the 'front line' and battery positions had to be 'recced' and occupied as part of the defensive plan. The batteries came into action in the area of In Seirat, with the O.P.s on high ground overlooking the Wadi and able to see, in the distance, their old friend Gaza "mocking . . . and smiling in the setting sun". For Eastern Force as a whole, the First Battle of Gaza was a resounding defeat but, like many other units, 270 Brigade emerged with credit, known within the division as Gunners who could be relied on, and with valuable experience of action. For them, the war had at last begun in earnest.

Under pressure from London for a success in the Egypt–Palestine theatre comparable with the capture of Baghdad on the Mesopotamian front, plans were made for a further advance and attack ('The Second Battle of Gaza'). Operations were to begin on 17th April, with a general advance from the line of the Wadi Guzze by the three infantry divisions assigned to the capture of Gaza (53rd Division with its left flank on the sea, 52nd Division in the centre and 54th with its right flank on the familiar ground of Sheikh Abbas). The two mounted divisions

Plate 49 *The Second Battle of Gaza, April 1917. Lieutenant E.J.T. Lutyens* (left), *acting as forward observation officer, and his signaller, in the barley fields over which part of the battle was fought.* (Regimental Collection)

would secure the British eastern flank, without attempting the encircling manoeuvre that had been impossible to supply with water during the earlier battle. An intervening day (18th April) would be used to complete preparations for the assault on Gaza by frontal attack, and for a heavy bombardment of the Turkish defences. The three weeks between the First and Second Battles of Gaza were of use to both sides – to the British for reconnaissance and for bringing forward additional troops and artillery, and to the Turks for strengthening, under German direction, the defences of Gaza, and for building a series of trench systems, or 'redoubts', that ran south-eastwards from Gaza, along the line of the Gaza–Beersheba road.

During the night of 16th–17th April 270 Brigade crossed the Wadi Guzze – a much easier proposition now that the crossing places had been improved – and came into action on the Sharta ridge in support of 162 Infantry Brigade, the left flank brigade in 54th Division's 'two-up' attack. At dawn on 17th April, 52nd and 54th Divisions, forming the 'Eastern Attack', "advanced without difficulty over ground thoroughly explored during the First Battle of Gaza" (*Official History*) and 54th Division had occupied its allotted objectives by 7.00 a.m. The brigade had not fired a shot but Second Lieutenant Lutyens, well ahead as a forward observation officer for A Battery, later reported that he ran out nearly five miles of wire. Late on 17th April 270 Brigade moved to positions between the Mansura and Sheikh Abbas features in preparation for the second phase of the attack. Registration of the next day's bombardment took place during 18th April and efforts were made to bring forward stocks of water and, of course, ammunition.

The heavy artillery bombardment opened at 05.30 a.m. on 19th April but the 18-pdrs. and 4.5-in. howitzers – the latter firing gas shell for the first time in the theatre – did not join in until 7.20 a.m., ten minutes before H-hour. There then started what the *Official History* describes as a "black day", during which 54th Division suffered very heavy casualties in their attack on the two Turkish redoubts on the Gaza–Beersheba road (known as 'Beer' and 'Tank', and described by Bullock as "formidable"). The preliminary bombardment proved ineffective, especially in failing to neutralise the enemy's artillery and machine-guns, and although the leading elements of both infantry brigades did get into the enemy positions, they were unable to effect a lodgement. At about 2.30 p.m., General Hare, commanding 54th Division, ordered his forward units to stand fast on the line they then held and, as nightfall approached, General Dobell confirmed the 'stand fast' order across the whole front, for nowhere had a significant break-through been achieved. During the night the attack was abandoned. A skilful and determined Turkish defence had held against the British "dogged advance against imperfectly located entrenchments and in the face of fire from hidden artillery, without adequate support from that arm on the side of the attackers" (*Official History*). Criticism of the part played by the artillery in the Second Battle of Gaza centres on the inadequate numbers of guns, especially those greater than field calibre, rather than on tactical handling or the efforts and achievements of individual brigades and batteries. The three batteries of 270 Brigade were in action all day and were fortunate to get through the day without casualties at the 'gun end' or amongst the forward observer parties. Major Lawrence of A Battery gained particular distinction (and a subsequent Mention in Despatches) when he observed a strong counter-attack developing against the vulnerable mile-wide gap between the left flank of 54th

[57]

Division's 162 Brigade and the right flank of 52nd Division. He established the range with a two-round 'bracket' and brought in all three batteries with "beautifully timed shrapnel (*through which*) the Turks gallantly advanced nearly another 1,500 yards before finally breaking into utter rout" (Griffith).

A third failure to capture Gaza could not be contemplated, nor indeed did it happen, but it was to be seven months before the advance was resumed. There would be a different commander and better resources, but above all, important changes would be made in the organisation of the whole force and in the measures for its command and control.

Chapter 5

Break-through and Follow-up

The Period of Waiting and Reorganisation, April–October 1917

After the failure at 'Second Gaza', Eastern Force did not, as in March, withdraw behind the Wadi Guzze, but stabilised its front line along the approximate positions held after the battle. From the sea west of Gaza town, the line ran south-eastwards to Sheikh Abbas and turned south to join the Wadi Guzze near Tell el Fara on the Rafa–Beersheba road. The Turks, on the other hand, reinforced the Gaza defences and their line of redoubts, establishing dominance over the whole Gaza–Beersheba line, though on their left flank Beersheba was lightly held compared with Gaza.

For some five weeks after the Second Battle of Gaza, 54th Division continued to hold the ground over which it had fought during the battle and the divisional artillery was occupied with the normal static-front tasks – registration of targets for possible future engagement, 'harassing fire' against known and suspected enemy positions, especially at night, and defensive fire planning. Command of 270 Brigade changed on 18th May 1917, when, to the delight of those officers and men who had known him as adjutant, Lieutenant-Colonel J.C. Dunbar returned to succeed Lieutenant-Colonel Sowler as commanding officer. On 25th May the brigade was withdrawn from its positions in support of 54th Division in the Mansura–Sheikh Abbas–Sharta sector of the front for rest and refitting near Deir el Belah. They returned to the front line on 12th June, but this time to positions well to the north-west of those previously occupied, for 54th Division had been moved to hold the extreme left of the British line, from the sea at Sheikh Ajlin for about two miles in a line a little south of south-east to include the feature known as Samson Ridge – not two hundred feet high but sufficient to dominate the enemy-held territory to the north and east and afford observation into the south-western outskirts of Gaza town. For the next four months B Battery occupied a position on cliffs by the sea. While claiming that "the nearness of the sea and the cool breeze which blew from it with unfailing regularity from midday to sunset" made this position the best in the whole line, Major Stanley continued:

> "The chief disadvantages were the absence of any cover from aeroplane observation, and the usual lack of water, every drop of which had to be brought up at night with the rations and ammunition from the wagon lines behind the Wadi Guzze, four-and-a-half miles away. The absence of cover necessitated the most scrupulous camouflage, everything having to be covered with sand and all shadows avoided . . .
>
> The only assistance provided by Nature was a scanty row of bushes about four feet high, extending for about twenty yards. All ranks lived in deep dug-outs with the entrances close to the bushes and carefully covered by day with sacking to hide the hole . . . The place became known as Milton Park (*an estate close to Peterborough which the battery used for weekend training in peacetime*) . . .
>
> The gun-pits were not in accordance with any known handbook but were evolved by experience. They consisted of an oval hole about three feet deep and just large enough to contain the gun and work it freely. A string net on light poles was spread over it and there was an underground chamber on each side. In one of these chambers the detachment lived, day and night, and in the other was stored the ammunition . . . The ground was deep, heavy sand and the only way to make a dug-out was to dig a hole about twice the size required and build strong sandbag walls in flemish bond and roof it with corrugated iron covered with more sandbags, finishing on the normal ground level or very little above it, with here and there a ventilator covered with a flap of sacking by day . . ."

Plate 50   *B Battery, 270 Brigade during the build-up to the Third Battle of Gaza.*
Top – The camouflaged gun position.
Bottom – Signallers' dugouts at 'Milton Park'.
The ever-present threats of air reconnaissance, bombing and counter-battery fire ensured high standards of camouflage and protection.
(Regimental Collection)

All three batteries prepared similar positions and began the routine of registration of targets and harassing fire. Two weeks after arrival in the new sector, Colonel Dunbar contracted diphtheria and was evacuated to hospital. Unusually, he was replaced almost at once by Lieutenant-Colonel J.C. Rea, but he was to return in due course, giving rise to an amusing incident that will be described later.

At the end of June 1917, General Sir Archibald Murray was replaced as commander-in-chief by General Sir Edmund Allenby. Once he had visited the forward areas and consulted his senior commanders, especially General Chetwode, who had taken over command of Eastern Force from General Dobell immediately after Second Gaza, the new Commander-in-Chief made important organisational changes. He split his own headquarters into two 'echelons', one of which would command future operations from a forward position, while the other, remaining in Cairo, would deal with a range of administrative matters and with the rule of Egypt under martial law. Headquarters Eastern Frontier Force (generally known as 'Eastern Force') was abolished and three corps headquarters – XX Corps, XXI Corps and Desert Mounted Corps – interposed between G.H.Q. and divisions. (This Army–Corps–Division chain of command was as practiced elsewhere, notably in France and Mesopotamia, and its introduction, with properly staffed headquarters, was to remove most of the command and control difficulties that had beset Eastern Force.) Three more infantry divisions were placed under command of the Egyptian Expeditionary Force – the 10th and 60th by transfer from Salonika and the 75th, which was formed in Egypt from a mixture of British and Indian units. Steps were also taken to increase the number of guns available to the Egyptian Expeditionary Force, both by bringing the remaining 4-gun field batteries up to 6-gun establishment and by increasing the number of medium and heavy batteries in the order of battle; methods were evolved by which, in the absence of fully staffed higher artillery headquarters, field brigade headquarters would co-ordinate the fire of several batteries, including medium and heavy; and brigade ammunition columns were removed from brigade command and reorganised into divisional ammunition columns.

July and August 1917 were months of somewhat reduced activity, owing partly to the summer heat and partly to the diversion of all forms of resource to the extension of the railways and water pipelines supplying the forward areas. There were, nevertheless, some important raids on the enemy's defensive system, both to gain intelligence and to maintain dominance and initiative along the front. The first of these raids in which 270 Brigade was involved took

Plate 51 *A party from A/270 watering their horses at wooden troughs laid out in the desert, summer 1917.* (Regimental Collection)

place during the night of 14th–15th July, when 1st/8th Hampshire Regiment, of 163 Infantry Brigade, raided 'Beach Post', an isolated Turkish strongpoint between the main Gaza defences and the sea. Two batteries of 44 Brigade, R.F.A. (from 74th Division) were placed under command of 270 Brigade for this operation and occupied positions behind the 54th Division front two nights prior to the raid, allowing registration of targets during 13th July. The infantry had carried out a rehearsal some days earlier and the raid was over within forty minutes, with a 'bag' of eighteen prisoners and one machine-gun for the cost of one killed and eight wounded. Messages of congratulation hailed the operation as a model of infantry–artillery co-operation.

No sooner had the Beach Post raid finished, than orders arrived for a raid on Umbrella Hill, a strongly held feature, slightly forward of the main Gaza defences and opposite 54th Division's right flank. The raid was to be carried out by 1st/5th Bedfordshire Regiment, of 162 Infantry Brigade, on the night of 20th–21st July. Captain Bailey's immediate impression on receiving details of the operation was that it was "a rather complicated affair" and he drew up an extra-large-scale map (1:5,000) on which to plot the various tasks. One additional battery – A/303, from 60th Division – was placed under command of 270 Brigade. On the night of 19th July, while preparations for the raid were in hand, Colonel Dunbar arrived back from hospital and resumed command of 270 Brigade for all purposes except the raid on Umbrella Hill the following night, which would be directed by Colonel Rea. The handover between commanding officers coincided with a strong Turkish attack on Samson Ridge – probably a large-scale raid. According to Captain Bailey, whose post in action was, of course, in the brigade headquarters:

> "When the Turks attacked both colonels assumed command and gave contrary orders. Fortunately, I managed to get to the telephone before either of them, but Dunbar roared orders into one ear and Rea yelled exactly opposite orders into the other. Dunbar was no doubt right in assuming command but unfortunately had been away so long that he was not up-to-date on the situation and had not read the latest orders on night lines, barrages, rates of fire, etc. I took no notice of either of them and commanded the brigade myself . . . It was the most ridiculous situation I have known. Luckily the Turks were repelled entirely by artillery fire before any of them reached our trenches."

The raid duly took place at 9.00 p.m. on 20th July and was over within fifty minutes. It was a great success, with more than one hundred enemy killed and seventeen prisoners. However, as the raiding party regained our lines, the Turks put down a tremendous barrage across their route, resulting in 24 men killed and more than eighty wounded, including Second Lieutenant J.W.A. Taylor of A/270, the forward observation officer with the raiding party. For their gallantry, skill and devotion to duty during the raid, Second Lieutenant Taylor was awarded the Military Cross and his signaller, Bombardier S.A. Craft, the Military Medal.

The routine continued throughout August and September, eased by two weeks' rest at Deir el Belah in mid-August and enlivened by further raids and increasing bombardment and harassing fire programmes. These tended to provoke a measure of counter-battery retaliation [61]

Plate 52   *A Battery's accommodation dugouts along a small wadi to the rear of the battery position, summer 1917.*
(Regimental Collection)

by the Turks and on 26th September C Battery was seriously hit for the second time. One of the 4.5-in. howitzers was put out of action by two direct hits and Second Lieutenant Symonds, who had been mentioned in despatches for his conduct when the battery was first hit in May, was seriously wounded. Now, his gallantry led to the award of the Military Cross.

The Third Battle of Gaza, October–November 1917

By the middle of October 1917, preparations for the resumption of the advance into Palestine were complete. The Commander-in-Chief issued orders on 22nd October for the Desert Mounted Corps and XX Corps to capture Beersheba, while XXI Corps (52nd, 54th and 75th Divisions) carried out a 'holding action' against Gaza town, which included a heavy artillery bombardment, designed to reinforce the Turks' appreciation that Gaza, not Beersheba, was the principal British objective. The bombardment plan, which reached 270 Brigade on about 8th October, was by far the most complex artillery operation yet carried out in the Egypt–Palestine theatre and the heaviest bombardment outside France. It involved 68 medium and heavy guns and the divisional artilleries of the three divisions of XXI Corps – 124 18-pdrs. and 4.5-in. howitzers – over a frontage of six thousand yards. The pressure in 270 Brigade Headquarters was considerable, though the brigade's participation in smaller fire plans covering raids provided valuable experience. On 11th October 1917 Captain Bailey noted:

> "Was doing the six-day show with the colonel all morning. The day of the attack is to be 'X-day' and the six days immediately preceding it will be known as 'X minus 6', 'X minus 5' and so on. 'X-day' is not yet fixed.
>
> We are arranging our six days' programme so that the whole of the front . . . is plastered all day and every day. Each battery is allotted certain 1,000-yard squares in which they are to engage targets at certain hours – the squares within which are the battery's bombardment

[62]

Plate 53 *Bathing parade for men and horses of A/270 in the sea near Deir el Belah.* (Regimental Collection)

targets for the final assault – in order that the registration of targets may be perfected during the six days. Each battery is also given certain hours each day and each night during which it will not fire and during which its personnel must rest.

As well as the day programme, I am working out night firing orders for each battery for each night . . ."

To ensure that every available battery was co-ordinated into the bombardment, whether or not it was in direct support of the attacking infantry, 'groups' of batteries were formed, each under the command of a brigade headquarters. 'No. 2 R.A. Group', based on Headquarters 270 Brigade, R.F.A. and consisting of A/270, C/270 and three batteries from 52nd Divisional Artillery, supported 163 Infantry Brigade, while B/270 formed part of No. 3 Group, supporting 161 Infantry Brigade, which was based on Headquarters 271 Brigade, R.F.A. A useful naval bombardment force assembled offshore. Their particular value was in their ability to steam up the coast and engage targets that were either out of range of the corps artillery or could not be seen from land-based observation posts. Royal Navy officers were attached to each R.A. group to maintain ship-to-shore liaison and to observe fire. Each field battery was ordered to prepare a position only a short distance behind the present front line, so that it could be occupied with the minimum of delay, and supporting fire could continue to be given to the infantry as they advanced out of range of the positions the batteries had occupied for so many weeks, and which they had used for the bombardment and initial attack phase. Ammunition in hitherto undreamed of quantities was available. Each gun had storage space for 1,000 rounds of ready-use ammunition dug in beside the gun pit. It would be needed, for to quote only one example, at one period during the bombardment A Battery was scheduled to fire 2,000 rounds in less than eight hours.

'X-Day' was eventually fixed for 2nd November and on X minus 6:

"The six days' bombardment started according to plan – not very intense to start with . . . walked up to the Naval O.P. to watch . . . Very interesting to see how it all 'pans out' after all the work and head scratching we have had about it. Rather like waiting for the marks of an examination paper to come out . . . A thunderstorm and very heavy rain started at 9.00 p.m. The heat was tremendous and the wet awful and at the batteries most of the gunners served their guns during the night firing clad only in towels.

X minus 5 – Bombardment a good deal more intense . . . Was in the office most of the afternoon. Paperwork has distinctly diminished now the show has started."

During the afternoon of X minus 1 (1st November), Headquarters 270 Brigade/No. 2 R.A. Group moved forward to its 'battle H.Q.', which had been prepared, at the expense of several days' digging, before the bombardment started.

The assault on Gaza, which began during the night of 1st–2nd November 1917 was carried out by 54th Division, reinforced by 156 Infantry Brigade of 52nd Division and with call on the whole of the artillery under XXI Corps command. The objectives, in four phases, comprised Umbrella Hill and the trench/redoubt systems stretching around the south-west and west of Gaza and through to Sheikh Hassan, a Turkish outpost on the coast nearly two miles from [63]

Plate 54 *C Battery's position before the Third Battle of Gaza. Top – 4.5-in. howitzer. Note the detail of the ped-rails on the gun wheels and the nickname 'Gaza Express' bestowed by the detachment. Bottom – The same gun put out of action by two direct hits from 5.9-in. counter-battery fire, 26th September 1917.*
(Regimental Collection)

54th Division's left flank positions just north of Sheikh Ajlin–Sheikh Ahmed. Zero hour for Phase 1 – the capture of Umbrella Hill, a necessary preliminary to further general advance – was at 11.00 p.m. on 1st November. After ten minutes of intense bombardment, which was successful in cutting the wire and neutralising enemy fire, 7th Scottish Rifles, of 156 Infantry Brigade, carried the position with remarkably light casualties.

Captain Bailey's diary records that on 2nd November (X-Day):

"Zero hour for Phase 2 was 3.00 a.m. The bombardment was simply terrific. We had several batteries just behind us, firing at short range over our heads, and the noise was absolutely deafening. It was one continuous roar and occasionally you could distinguish an individual round from a battery close behind. The enemy machine-guns simply poured stuff over. An orderly standing outside a dugout at Battle H.Q. (*evidently Gunner S.C. Boyce – see Hertfordshire Yeomanry and Artillery Roll of Honour*) was shot through the head. We tried to do what we could for him but he died almost at once."

On 163 Infantry Brigade's front, heavy Turkish defensive fire and the dark night were responsible for some confusion and loss of direction but on the right 5th Suffolks and their neighbouring battalion of 156 Infantry Brigade, 4th Royal Scots, kept close behind No. 2 Group's barrage and over-ran El Arish Redoubt after fierce hand-to-hand fighting but with few losses to themselves. The left-hand battalion, 8th Hampshire, captured its objective, Burj Trench, but 4th and 5th Norfolks, following through to the Third Phase objectives 'Crested Rock' and 'Gibraltar', failed to secure them.

Meanwhile, on the left of 54th Division, No. 3 Group, which included B/270, were in direct support of 161 Infantry Brigade, attacking along the coast with objectives 'Sea Post', 'Beach Post' and 'Rafah Redoubt'. Major Stanley noted:

"Target time-tables detailing minutely each battery's work in the bombardment had been issued in good time and we had prepared in elaboration of the idea an exact time-table for each round for each gun, so that I had nothing to do after the first round was fired except walk about and wonder how the infantry were getting on. I remember feeling extraordinarily 'out of it' and idle . . .

The battery's particular programme commenced with a ten minute bombardment of Sea Post, lifting from there to a communication trench, and then to other fire trenches, trench junctions, etc., beyond, timed to allow the infantry to reach each point just as the guns lifted and to protect them in their advance to the next, ending with a creeping barrage through Sheikh Hasan wood, the guns increasing the range fifty yards every few minutes and the infantry following the bursting shells.

The enemy's barrage came down within a very few minutes of our opening fire, but, as our infantry were by that time half-way across No Man's Land, it fell harmlessly behind them. Our bombardment and barrage time-table lasted for about three hours, and as everything seemed to be going well, I went up to Ajlin O.P. as soon as it was getting light, to see what was to be seen. That was very little. Sea Post and Beach Post were now flatter than ever, and the wire was in shreds everywhere; but the battle was away out of sight over Sheikh Hasan wood, beyond which my shells were now bursting in a slow, protective barrage, pending orders to cease fire".

There had, in fact, been some confusion and loss of direction on the right of the 161 Infantry Brigade attack, which resulted in the troops which should have passed through to more distant objectives becoming involved in heavy and confused fighting before Rafah Redoubt fell. On the left, 6th Essex secured Sea Post and Beach Post with only light casualties, and eventually Cricket Redoubt was captured with the help of a tank – one of very few in the theatre – brought up from Beach Post.

The way was now clear for 162 Infantry Brigade to move through 161 Brigade to the final objective, Sheikh Hasan. On their extreme right, 10th London became mixed up in the clearance of Rafah Redoubt (see above). In the centre there was a sharp struggle for 'Gun Hill', but by 6.00 a.m. (at about the time Major Stanley began to watch the battle) the brigade was ready for the assault on Sheikh Hasan and, after fifteen minutes' bombardment, secured the area

Plate 55 *Lieutenant W.G. Barford, gun position officer of B Battery, giving orders to his guns, September–October 1917. To his left is the camouflaged entrance to the command post dug-out. Telephone wires emerge from the sand and are secured to a tapping-in point, while an 18-pdr. cartridge case has been mounted for use as an alarm gong.*
(Regimental Collection)

54th DIVISIONAL ARTILLERY   Copy No /4

Reference GAZA 1/20,000   WARNING ORDER NO 1.

3/10/17

INTENTION. (1)   The 54th Division plus one Infantry Bde 52nd Division is to attack the hostile front from CAIRO ROAD to The SEA.

The above attack will be supported by the 54th and 52nd Divisional Artilleries.

The attack will be carried out by three Infantry Bdes supported by one Artillery Group as follows:-

The 155th Infantry Brigade supported by No 1 R.A. Group will attack from CAIRO ROAD to a line ran through P 26 b 7.7 and P 26 c 1.6.

The 163rd Infantry Bde supported by No 2 R.A. Group will attack thence to a line drawn from ZOWAIID TRENCH (exclusive) to JONES POST.

The 161st Infantry Bde supported by No 3 R.A. Group will attack thence to the SEA.

GROUPING   (2)   The 54th and 52nd Divisional Artilleries will be grouped as under:-

No 1 Group. Lieut Col J.FARQUHAR D.S.O.

A/281st Bde R.F.A.
B/261st Bde R.F.A.
C/261st Bde R.F.A.
B/262nd Bde R.F.A.

No 2 Group   Lieut Col J.C.DUNBAR D.S.O.

A/270th Bde R.F.A.
C/270th Bde R.F.A.
A/264th Bde R.F.A.
A/262nd Bde R.F.A.
C/264th Bde R.F.A.

No 3 Group   Lieut Col R.H.LAURIE D.S.O.

A/271st Bde R.F.A.
B/271st Bde R.F.A.
B/270th Bde R.F.A.
B/272nd Bde R.F.A.
C/272nd Bde R.F.A.

Positions of Batteries, O.P.s, etc will be as shown on attached Schedule "D".

ZERO DAY. (3)   The day of the Infantry assault will be known as Zero day.

Plate 56   *The Third Battle of Gaza, November 1917. The first page of the 'warning order' issued by H.Q.R.A. 54th Division on 3rd October, which outlines the intention (Para. 1) and gives details of the three artillery groups formed from the fourteen batteries of the 52nd and 54th Divisional Artilleries (Para. 2). Lieutenant-Colonel J.C. Dunbar, with Brigade Headquarters of 270 Brigade took command of No. 2 Group.*

[66]   (Regimental Collection)

VERY SECRET.

Ref.1/20,000
GAZA.

54th D.A. WARNING ORDER No 1.

18 pdr BARRAGE TIME TABLE PHASE I

Schedule A. Sheet 2.

AMENDED

Time.	Unit.	Target.	Rds.	Remarks.
0 to plus 10'	LE	Front line UMBRELLA HILL Right portion P 33 c 6.7 to c 3.7	120	Lifts 200 yards at Plus 10'
	MM	" " " " Centre portion P 33 c 3.7 to c 1.8	180	
	LP	" " " " Left portion P 33 c 1.8 to P 33 a 0.0	180	
	MF	Support trench P 33 a 1.1 to a 3.0	180	Lifts 100 yards at plus 10'
	LG	DUG OUT ALLEY	60	Switches at plus 10'
	LU	4 Guns on front line EL ARISH REDOUBT from P 26 b 6.3 to b 9.1 2 " " " " P 27 c 5.8 to 9.8	120	
Plus 10' to plus 28'	LE	Lifts a further 100 yds at plus 15' and establishes barrage P 33 a 8.4 to b 0.3 at plus 20'	72	
	MM	Lifts to barrage trench P 33 b 0.3 to b2 2, slight switch req'd.	108	
	LP	Lifts to barrage trench P 33 b 2.2 to d 4.9	108	
	MF	Lifts a further 100 yards at plus 15' and establishes barrage P 33 a 6.7 to a 8.4 at plus 30'	108	
	LG	Switches to barrage trench Junction at P 33 a 8.4	36	
	LU	As Phase I	108	
Plus 28' to plus 100'	LE) LG)	Barrages P 27 d 35.20 to d 6.0	288	Will come under direct orders of Inf Brigadier at plus 100'
	MF	Barrages P 27 d 1.4 to d 35.20	288	
	MM	Barrages from P 27 d 6.0 to p 33 b 7.8	288	
	LP	Barrages from P 33 b 7.8 to P 33 b 95.60	288	
	LU	As Phase 1.	288	
		Fire in this period will be stopped if found not required.		

Plate 57 *The Third Battle of Gaza, November 1917. Part of the 'Barrage Time Table' for the first phase of the battle. The table would be readily recognisable by a present-day Gunner officer or command post assistant, though the method of indicating the targets on the map differs markedly from today's grid references.* (Regimental Collection)

with little difficulty, taking nearly two hundred prisoners. There were three separate Turkish counter-attacks during 2nd November, all in strength, but they were beaten off by fire from the British medium and heavy artillery and the naval bombardment group. The *Official History* concluded that while the attack on the western defences of Gaza had not reached all its objectives – the most serious failure being on 163 Infantry Brigade's front, where Crested Rock and Gibraltar, which would have provided invaluable artillery O.P.s for No. 1 Group, remained in enemy hands – the Commander-in-Chief's overall intentions had been realised.

To the west of Gaza, there was little activity by either side during the four days immediately following X-Day. In between occasional Turkish bombardments and No.1 Group's responses, officers found time to visit the new front line and inspect at close quarters positions they had observed, and shelled, for several months previously. Captain Bailey and an officer named Spalding, who was temporarily attached to Headquarters No.1 Group, "crawled out into No Man's Land and got a grand view by lying on top of a little knoll". They were spotted, however, and were fired on by a Turkish battery, so beat a hasty retreat, after which, "Spalding took my photo . . . complete with tin hat, gas mask, etc." (Steel helmets had reached the Egypt–Palestine theatre only a few days before the Third Battle of Gaza, and an order was in force that they were to be worn by all troops on the Gaza side of the Wadi Guzze.) The opportunity to sleep for more than an hour or so at one time was welcomed by the diarists and Captain Bailey recorded on 5th November (X+4), ". . . quite a quiet day – both sides rather regaining breath".

In fact, the initiative lay with General Allenby. On 6th November, XX Corps advanced to the capture of the Turkish positions around Tel esh Sheria, some twenty miles south-east of Gaza, and the Commander-in-Chief ordered the Desert Mounted Corps to manoeuvre to cut off Gaza by a right hook towards the coast. The advance of the Desert Mounted Corps on 7th November would be assisted by renewed attacks on the southern and western defences of [67]

Gaza by 54th and 75th Divisions of XXI Corps. As far as B/270 were concerned, preparations for the attack on 7th November began after dark on 5th November, when they moved forward about one thousand yards to occupy a position behind the old Sheikh Ahmed O.P., ready to support 161 Infantry Brigade in their attack, with 162 Brigade, on 'Turtle Hill', immediately north-west of Gaza town. Major Stanley described how, on 6th November, he had "a thoroughly amusing time . . . registering for the bombardment programme which was to precede the coming attack". Then:

> "Two hours before dawn on 7th November the inferno of the 2nd was repeated and, as we were now on higher ground, the uproar seemed greater than ever; the rattle of hundreds of machine-guns, the barking of the 18-pounders and the booming of the heavies behind us made up a concert that will always be unforgettable. As dawn broke, the programme came to an end and for the first time for many days and nights there was absolute quiet. The Turks had gone. The stillness was weird. The news soon came through that the infantry had walked straight over, occupied all the objectives, and found that Gaza was evacuated."

The Advance into Palestine and the First Action on the Nahr el Auja, November–December 1917

While 52nd Division pushed through the gaps created by the successful reduction of Gaza and pursued the retreating Turks with the immediate objective of preventing them from making a stand on the Wadi el Hesi – a potentially strong defensive position about seven miles to the north – 54th Division were left, literally, as 'masters of the battlefield'. Largely denuded of transport, lent to reinforce the 'pursuit' formations, the division had several days of enforced immobility in bivouac close to the coast south and west of Gaza town. The divisional artillery was assigned the task of salvaging useable ammunition, great quantities of

[68]

which were still in pits on gun positions vacated by batteries of 52nd Division, as well as in their own positions and in dumps to the rear. Captain Bailey spent a lot of time supervising this recovery operation and making arrangements for disposal of the ammunition, while still being able to visit Gaza and prominent features of the former Turkish front line, until, on 13th November, 270 Brigade received "orders and counter-orders about a possible move forward tomorrow".

The pursuit formations made good progress, and by 19th November Desert Mounted Corps were holding a line from the sea just north of Jaffa, along the south bank of the Nahr el Auja to Tel Abu Zeitun and thence south-eastwards through El Yehudiye to Nalin. On the afternoon of 14th November, 54th Division had indeed moved out of the Gaza area and trekked by easy stages to reach Desert Mounted Corps on 20th November and begin taking over the El Yehudiye–Nalin sector of the line two days later. Before leaving Gaza, 270 Brigade had exchanged their summer khaki drill uniforms and sun helmets for serge uniforms and caps, and on 19th November they dumped the ped-rails, having concluded that they were now "definitely off sand". Their appearance on the march had accordingly changed considerably.

During the night of 23rd–24th November, the Australian and New Zealand Mounted Division was ordered to seize a bridgehead across the Nahr el Auja in order to induce the Turks to believe that the advance was continuing along the coast. The New Zealand Mounted Brigade was selected to carry out the operation and, in the absence of adequate artillery support, 270 Brigade (less B Battery) was placed under command of the Australian and New Zealand Mounted Division and in direct support of the brigade. Having seized the bridgehead, it was planned that the New Zealand brigade would be relieved by 161 Infantry Brigade (less two battalions). The *Official History* makes clear how swiftly this operation was mounted; Captain Bailey is more graphic in his description of the events of 24th November:

". . . rode into Jaffa with Dunbar to a conference at A.N.Z. Mounted Division H.Q. They decided to have a battle at once – no orders were issued at all. We were just told vaguely to go and bombard a certain bridge over the Nahr el Auja while the mounted troops went round by a ford at the mouth of the river and attacked the garrison of the bridge from behind. There was no time-table. We were to stop firing when we saw the leading troops coming.

I galloped as hard as I could all the way back to Selmeh to get the brigade on the move. They moved at 11.00 a.m. I changed horses and led the brigade to meet Dunbar, who had gone straight to the hills to the north to select battery positions for the battle. We went into action and shelled the bridgehead from 1.00 p.m. to 3.30 p.m. We had to go pretty easy with ammunition as we did not have much. The mounted troops came round and took the bridge according to plan, doing a most spectacular charge over a little hill behind the bridge. It was a capital battle! We captured 25 Turks and two machine-guns, and nobody was killed on either side."

Plate 59   *The 4.5-in. howitzers of C/270 in action, late 1917–early 1918. The absence of camouflage and gun pits suggests that this photograph was taken during the mobile phase of operations following the Third Battle of Gaza.* (Regimental Collection)

The operation had been a little more complex than Bailey recorded, but no less successful, having taken the enemy completely by surprise. The Canterbury Regiment secured the crossing and pressed on some two miles to occupy the hamlet of Muwannis. The Wellington Regiment then followed through to secure the higher ground at Hadra, a further two miles to the east. It was the Wellington Regiment, supported by 3 Light Armoured Motor Battery, who had carried out the 'spectacular charge' to the bridge, observed by Captain Bailey. By late afternoon, 6th and 4th Essex of 161 Infantry Brigade were taking over Muwannis and Hadra respectively, from the New Zealanders, four squadrons of whom maintained an outpost screen across nearly five miles of bridgehead as night fell. Surprisingly, 270 Brigade was 'stood down' and went into bivouac at Sarona, between Jaffa and the river. Only one 4-gun battery – the Somerset R.H.A. – remained in action in support of the outposts and the two companies each of the Essex battalions that were north of the river.

According to the *Official History*, "The Turks quickly gave proof that they did not intend to permit the establishment of a bridgehead". At 4.15 a.m. on 25th November enemy concentrations were observed north-east of Hadra and some minutes later the Turks began their advance, accompanied by a heavy bombardment of the Hadra position. Captain Bailey recorded:

"We were woken up in our bivouac at the first streak of dawn by a lot of firing. I got up and went to talk to Dunbar. Just as I was writing a message to Headquarters A.N.Z. Division to say that we were going out with a section of guns to stop the noise, a motorcycle despatch rider came rushing into camp at a tremendous pace over the grass with an urgent message saying 'Heavily attacked; reoccupy yesterday's positions at once to support'. We immediately had a battery commanders' conference in pyjamas, and ordered 'Boot and Saddle' at once. In exactly seventy minutes from receiving the message we had both batteries (A/270 and C/270) in action in their previous day's positions, over four thousand yards from the bivouac, and both batteries had opened fire.

The enemy attacked in force (about 6,000) and drove our infantry out of Hadra and all the ground won yesterday, and finally drove them back across the Auja itself. We observed for our batteries from a very high hill (map reference 'Z.30'), which became generally known as Z.30. We were in action all day and were running very short of ammunition. I rode back to try to arrange for some to come up and fixed a place for a small dump. One of our battery wagons had been overturned by shellfire on the way into action, and another team had been hit. The enemy's shell fire was extraordinarily accurate as we came across the open into action, and also afterwards, when they shelled the top of Z.30 . . .

The Turks attacked all day and we had some very nice, long range, but I think very effective, enfilade fire at them as they occupied Muwannis. Later in the day we saw another Turkish force cross the River Auja further up to our right, not far from Mulebbis and it looked very much as if our right flank would be turned . . ."

The situation was clearly serious and no available guns could be left idle. B/270, concentrated with 163 Infantry Brigade at Ramleh, were sent for to rejoin A and C Batteries. Major Stanley later recalled.

"The battery was ordered to make a forced march from Ramleh to reinforce, and so, hastily resuming steel helmets, and leaving the first-line wagons to follow at a less hurried pace, the firing battery made a dash of about ten miles, luckily on a good road for once, but by the time the scene of action was reached the position was restored."

The *Official History* confirms that, "by the time the two remaining battalions of 161 Infantry Brigade had moved up from Sarona, any danger there may have been of the enemy obtaining a footing south of the Auja was over". In surveying the set-back of 25th November, it counts the decision to move 270 Brigade back to bivouac on the evening of the 24th as a "defect". The decision would not, of course, have been made by 270 Brigade, but the Official Historian is less than generous to the brigade's efforts once the Turkish attack had started, claiming that it "arrived on the scene of action . . . too late to be of much service", and that, as a result, the whole artillery defence . . . (*rested*) upon a single horse artillery battery". Without detracting from the very gallant performance of the Somerset R.H.A., the part played by A/270 and C/270 deserves greater recognition.

Late on 25th November, Colonel Dunbar was ordered back to Headquarters A.N.Z. Mounted Division and placed in command of an ad-hoc artillery group covering the twelve miles of front from the sea just south of the mouth of the Auja, eastwards to Tel Abu Zeitun and then south-east to El Yehudiye. 'R.A. Left Sector', as the group was designated, comprised all three batteries of 270 Brigade, five horse artillery batteries, one battery and one section of heavy artillery and two anti-aircraft sections. The whole totalled 46 guns of six different calibres, which, commented Captain Bailey, who accompanied Colonel Dunbar as brigade major, "complicated the question of ammunition". The Turks attacked again on 27th November as part of their efforts to defend Jerusalem. By far the greater part of these operations took place east of the Lydda–Haifa railway, but on their right flank they attempted to push south-westwards from Mulebbis. The battle was visible from Z.30, where Colonel Dunbar had, for the time being, established his tactical headquarters. His brigade major noted that, when Colonel Dunbar was ordered to return to divisional headquarters, "the situation on Z.30 looked pretty bad . . . Our howitzer battery (*C/270*) had one section firing in one direction and the other section with a line of fire exactly 180° different, both at ranges of less than three thousand yards". Once more, the situation was brought under control and fortunately, for it was the key to observation across several miles of the front, Z.30 remained in A.N.Z. hands. On 30th November, four days into this period of fighting, Colonel Dunbar had the opportunity of taking a captured officer (an Armenian) up to the O.P. on Z.30 and getting him to point out the Turkish positions. Activity on the front continued, with sizeable raids on the Turkish front line along the Auja and on 'Bald Hill', opposite the right of the A.N.Z. line. There was a lot of counter-battery work too, conducted by Major Lawrence from Z.30 and using the heavy sections as well as the batteries of 270 Brigade. In certain lights the smoke of Turkish guns could be observed and fire could swiftly be brought down upon them. Major Lawrence later claimed that he had mastery of all Turkish gun positions on his frontage except two. The workload in the ad-hoc H.Q.R.A. Left Sector was considerable, and another officer had to be brought in (from the Somerset R.H.A.) to take over 'A and Q' duties from Captain Bailey, leaving him to concentrate on 'G' matters (i.e., Operations). On 4th December the recce parties from 52nd Divisional Artillery arrived. The division was due to take over the line from A.N.Z. Mounted Division as part of a considerable rearrangement prior to the attack on Jerusalem, and while Colonel Dunbar showed the incoming C.R.A. around the battery positions and O.P.s, Captain Bailey wrote the orders for the relief, which took place on 7th December.

Colonel Dunbar resumed command of 270 Brigade, which remained in action in support of what Major Stanley described as a "thin and severely-tried line of posts held by the New Zealand Mounted Rifles". B Battery's position was:

". . . One of the nastiest positions the battery ever had . . . The country was mostly uncultivated, undulating veldt, covered with the dried-up grass of the previous summer and short scrub. There was no place for an O.P. that gave a good view or was not dominated by Bald Hill. Directly the steel helmets of any of the battery's officers or signallers were spotted by the observers on Bald Hill entering any of the New Zealanders' posts they were at once shelled, for they could guess their identity from the helmets; the New Zealanders were, of course, wearing their wide-brimmed hats . . .

From sunset to sunrise the air was thick with bullets, for the two chains of posts were fairly close and the Turk sniper at night had only one thought – to loose off his rifle once a minute to try to keep his opposite number's head down, or his own courage up . . . At any rate, most of his shots must have been far too high, for they simply peppered the battery position. After dark it was unsafe to move out of cover, which was in any case very difficult to acquire. Any hole one dug filled with water, and sand bags were very scarce indeed. Gunner Sharman was killed by a bullet clean though his eye as he slept, and one or more men were wounded every night."

The misery of the cold and the rain that filled B Battery's dug-outs and fell without stopping for three days was recorded, too, by Captain Bailey. Fortunately, on leaving the A.N.Z. Mounted Division, he and Colonel Dunbar had called at the Jerusalem Hotel in Jaffa before rejoining 270 Brigade and had bought "several dozen bottles of Médoc". Officers and men of brigade headquarters were thus able to resort to drinking "mulled Médoc" in their attempts to keep warm. The rain stopped on 10th December and, as they dried out, the brigade received

REF MAP I
INCH = 1 MILE
SHEET XIII

Left Sector Artillery Order 2.   2-12-17   Copy 1.

1. The Horse and Field Artillery of the Left Sector will be reorganised into three artillery Subsectors, named A B + C, each under the command of an Artillery Subsector Commander as follows :—

A Subsector Artillery covering Nos 1 and 2 Subsectors from YEHUDIYEH to Z30d.

Commander : Major D.E. C Stanley,

Artillery :- B/270
A/HAC
Essex Bty RHA

B Subsector Artillery covering No 3 Subsector from Z30d to NAHR EL BARIDEH

Commander :- Major G. Lawrence

Artillery :- A/270
C/270

C Subsector Artillery covering No 4 Subsector from NAHR EL BARIDEH to the sea

Commander :- Major M Clowes MC

Artillery :- 18th Bde RHA Somerset Bty
Inverness Bty
Ayrshire Bty

2. Somerset Bty RHA
A Bty HAC
Essex Bty RHA   will remain in their
A/270   present positions
C/270

The batteries mentioned on Schedule A attached will move in accordance with that schedule on the dates indicated.

3 18th Brigade Ammunition Column will move on the night of 4th/5th from SELMEH to H36c No 1 Section 54th DAC and Essex BAC will take over and maintain the signal office at SELMEH, under arrangements to be made by O.C No 1 Section 54th DAC.

4 Completion of all moves will be notified to this office by wire, by the O.C artillery Subsector into which the move takes place.

Plate 60   'Left Sector Artillery Order No. 2' in Captain Bailey's handwriting, issued on 2nd December 1917. The reorganisation of Left Sector into three sub-sectors was due to take place during the nights of 4th–5th and 5th–6th December and was designed to place all three 13-pdr. batteries of 18 Brigade, R.H.A. on the left of the sector ready to support an advance which it was anticipated would be made across the ford at the mouth of the Nahr el Auja. The redeployment may not have taken place, for recce parties from 52nd Divisional Artillery arrived on 4th December and on 7th December 52nd Infantry Division took over the line held by A.N.Z. Mounted Division.   (Regimental Collection)

two pieces of good news – Jerusalem had been captured, and they were to revert to command of 54th Division, being placed in direct support of 162 Infantry Brigade. Their battery positions would be around Kefr Ana, about seven miles south-east of Jaffa.

The Battle of Jaffa, December 1917

Headquarters XXI Corps had by now returned to the coastal plain and 75th Division had moved up to take over the line on the right of 54th Division. The 'original' XXI Corps (52nd, 54th and 75th Divisions) had thus been re-formed and stood once more with its left flank on the sea. With Jerusalem now in our hands, though not yet entirely safe from counter-attack, the push along the coast could be resumed, with the particular intention of securing Jaffa, which was still within range of the enemy's artillery, for use as a port. In a preparatory move, on 15th December, 54th and 75th Divisions pushed the right half of the corps frontage north-eastwards on to favourable ground just beyond the line Et Tire–Ibanne. The guns of 270 Brigade appear not to have been involved – they would have been at extreme range if, indeed, they had been able to give any support at all to 54th Division's assault brigade, 163 Infantry Brigade. However, officers were able to help by observing from the flank of the attack – probably at about right-angles to the line of fire – and directing the fire of the medium and heavy guns whose own O.P.s were unsighted by intervening crests. With his centre and right secure as a result of this limited operation, the corps commander could now concentrate on the advance along the coast.

What was subsequently known as the 'Battle of Jaffa' began on the night of 20th–21st December 1917, when, in a boldly executed night operation, 52nd Division crossed the Nahr el Auja. During 21st December they regained all the ground lost a month earlier, establishing a new line some two miles north of the river. The following night, 21st–22nd December, 162 Infantry Brigade secured Yafa Hill and the now infamous Bald Hill, their operations being supported by 270 Brigade. The capture of Bald Hill, now heavily fortified as part of the enemy's line, owed much to the tactics employed by 162 Infantry Brigade. Observing that the Turks expected attack from the south-west and had arranged their defences accordingly, General Hare, commanding 54th Division, ordered that Bald Hill should be approached from the south-east. To establish the start line for the attack in a suitable place, the brigade occupied a hill 350 yards east of the objective during the night of 20th–21st December and held it undetected throughout the next day. Major Stanley later described the battle for Bald Hill:

> "The orders for the battery were to commence a bombardment of the left half of Bald Hill at midnight (*21st–22nd December*) and to be prepared to advance at any moment after that to a position previously selected, close up to the infantry front line, which had been already wired for telephone. The 11th London Regiment were to make the attack on the hill. They were very short of men and the commanding officer was only a captain, so great had been their losses, but they were very gallant fellows. The Turks anticipated our attack by commencing a very heavy shelling of the posts and the country behind them (*i.e., the 54th Division area*) about 7.00 p.m. and this continued with considerable intensity far into the night. At midnight our bombardment programme was commenced and the Londons charged up the eastern slopes of Bald Hill, taking the trenches in enfilade. They met with very stiff resistance and the fight for the hill with bomb and bayonet lasted for several hours . . . Simultaneously, a slow barrage was put down on the communication trenches on the reverse of the hill to prevent, or make it, at any rate, unpleasant for, any reserves coming up. The Londons got the upper hand after an all-night struggle, and at about 8.30 a.m., as the Northamptons were passing through the battery on their way forward, the welcome message came over the wire from brigade headquarters . . . A word to the wagon lines one thousand yards away, where the drivers had been standing by their horses all night, and the battery was soon thundering forward in the bright winter sunshine, galloping in best R.H.A. fashion, to be in at the death if possible."

Indeed, according to the *Official History*, "At dawn on 22nd December it was seen that the enemy's guns and transport were everywhere moving northward, and when the general advance began at 8.00 a.m. there was no serious resistance". The 54th Division quickly pushed eastwards with 161 and 162 Infantry Brigades 'up' and secured a line from Ferrikhiye, on the south bank of the Auja, southwards through Fajja, then across the railway at Wilhelma Station to a point north-east of Et Tire. On the coast, 52nd Division made a further advance, with the result that, "The objects of the whole operation had been attained, and at very small cost. Jaffa was put out of range of artillery . . . and the British had a very favourable line".

After shelling the retreating enemy until he was out of range, the batteries of 270 Brigade moved into positions near Mulebbis. Christmas followed almost at once and, in a generous gesture, the people of Mulebbis decorated their village hall with palm branches and paper flowers and made it available for Christmas services. A service of Holy Communion was held at 6.30 a.m. on Christmas Day, followed by church parade at 8.30, both under a large red and white 'Welcome' notice. (The inhabitants of Mulebbis were Jewish and evidently were expressing a feeling of liberation.) While the spiritual side of Christmas was thus more than adequately provided for, the usual celebratory meal was more difficult to come by. Major Stanley later recalled that:

"... fate decreed that on Christmas Day 1917 the issue was half a ration of (*frozen*) rabbit, half a ration of biscuit, and no vegetables or jam. Plum puddings from home ... were said to be immovable ... somewhere or other. Two men with sacks and a handful of piastres were sent to scour the village. They managed to procure a quantity of cabbages, dates and black bread, and that resourceful person, the battery cook, produced a few carefully hoarded tins. Whatever they felt, the men showed the same splendid spirit with which they met every trial. The hardest thing to bear was that A Battery had somehow raised a pig!"

Not to be outdone by the batteries, Captain Bailey arranged for a water-carrying camel to go down to the local wine merchant and fill up with a more interesting cargo – they had White Port, Médoc and Sauternes. To crown everything, it rained all day. Christmas 1917 was, according to the *Official History*, "the climax to a period of nightmare for the services of supply". The railway had been washed away in places and storms at sea prevented the landing of supplies by boat. All the animals were on half rations too. Fortunately, this situation would not last more than a few days.

Chapter 6

Pursuit and Victory

Winter Standstill, December 1917–March 1918

It was now judged that renewed operations were out of the question until the rainy season had finished and railhead had moved a good deal closer to the front. Efforts were accordingly made to reorganise the defences along the 54th Division front, so as to give a greater measure of comfort and protection from the weather to both men and animals, while maintaining a sound defensive line. In accordance with a new operation order, 270 Brigade moved between 27th–30th December from Mulebbis to positions in the olive groves just north of Yehudie. Houses and barns were taken over for use as cookhouses, workshops and stores in the batteries' wagon lines; B Battery even managed a "covered stable for sick horses". The village of Yehudie had been deserted by its inhabitants, with the inevitable result that 'scrounging' parties from the brigade very quickly stripped the place of all types of wood- or metal-work that were likely to make dugouts and bivouacs more habitable in the conditions brought about by "Rain all day", which was the recurrent diary entry. As the rainy season wore on, the weather changed to alternate periods of about four days and nights of continuous rain, followed by six or seven days of beautiful spring sunshine.

The relative relaxation and good humour of the two-and-a-half months spent near Yehudie was marred in the early stages by a very unfortunate accident in which Lieutenant Davies of B Battery lost his life. Ordered to attend a course at Zeitoun in Egypt, Davies was being driven, with his servant, Gunner Weston, to railhead in a 4-horse cart under the command of Bombardier W.G. Blades. While crossing a swollen wadi, the cart overturned and all the occupants were thrown into the torrent. Davies and Blades struggled to the bank and then saw that Weston, who could not swim, was clinging to the upturned cart. Both men at once entered the water with the intention of bringing Weston to safety, which Blades succeeded in doing; Davies was swept away by the current and drowned. After running some distance along the bank in search of Davies but being forced to give up, Blades returned to the scene of the accident. He once more plunged into the torrent and succeeded in cutting away the two horses that were still alive and getting them to safety. In recognition of his great bravery on this occasion, Bombardier Blades was awarded the Royal Humane Society's Bronze Medal for Saving Life, while the Society's 'In Memoriam' Certificate was awarded to commemorate Lieutenant Davies' efforts at rescue, which cost him his life.

The monotony of this period, which was technically 'in the line', rather than 'in reserve', yet was almost totally inactive as far as the guns were concerned, was broken by self-help and ingenuity. Jackal hunting provided "excellent sport" (Stanley), and probably not just for the officers. A series of race meetings was organised on a course largely constructed by the brigade. At the divisional meeting on 2nd February 1918, Captain Bailey won the two-mile steeplechase open to officers of 54th Division by the handsome margin of three hundred yards, to the satisfaction of many members of 270 Brigade, who had backed him out of loyalty, rather than after a close study of form, to find they were pocketing quite reasonable winnings. (Two days later, Captain Bailey received a note from G.O.C. 54th Division suggesting that he should not ride his horse *Rex* in any future race open only to the division because they could field "nothing to compete with him" from within!). The next steeplechase meeting, open to the whole of XXI Corps, took place on 18th February. Captain Bailey and *Rex*, both of whom had been in serious training for two weeks, were given a 7-lb. penalty but nevertheless managed to win by 150 yards, once more to the satisfaction of the backers. Before his next race – the 'Palestine Grand National' on 28th February – *Rex* suffered a bout of colic. Though pronounced fit to run, he was evidently not quite in top form and fell at the last fence when [75] leading by half a length. The backers' disappointment was tempered, however, by Captain Bailey's performance with his other horse, *The Ghost*. in the 'Umbrella Stakes', a four-furlong flat race. After two false starts and in a field of nineteen, *The Ghost* was beaten into second place by a horse which pulled across his path some six strides from the finish. Mindful that "Everyone in the brigade had backed *The Ghost*", Captain Bailey lodged an objection, which was at once upheld.

While racing takes prominence in Captain Bailey's diary, it is evident from Major Stanley's that concert parties and theatricals were popular, as were sports meetings, for both athletic and mounted sports. The latter led to the discovery within B Battery of "quite an exceptional show jumper in a roan horse usually ridden by the staff-sergeant farrier (and one of the most uncomfortable brutes to ride), which afterwards won easily against the whole division". Beside all this fun and games, more serious affairs like the brigade turn-out competition fell a bit flat; there is a hint of disappointment, too, in the record that "C/270 were third" in the 54th Divisional Artillery best turn-out competition.

The Advance to Majdal Yaba, March 1918

"With the return of permanent sunshine at the beginning of March," Major Stanley wrote, "the wonderful flowers of Palestine made their appearance . . ." But good weather signalled the return of the campaigning season, too. Planning and preparation for what would later be officially described as the 'Actions of Tel Asur' had begun in the last few days of February. The overall intention was to advance the right of XXI Corps beyond the Wadi Abu Lejja–Wadi Deir Ballut, thus pushing out the 'Wilhelma Salient' which protruded southwards into the British line. One brigade of 54th Division on the left and two brigades of 75th Division on the right would advance northwards to secure the line Ras el Ain–Majdal Yaba–Deir Ballut. The plan relied heavily on the use of artillery, both in direct support of the assaulting brigade, 162 Infantry Brigade, and through enfilade fire from behind 54th Division's existing front line, which ran approximately parallel with the line of advance. The equivalent of four-and-a-half batteries of medium and heavy artillery was placed in support of 54th Division. Two batteries of 272 Brigade joined 270 Brigade in direct support of 162 Infantry Brigade, which, if all went well, would mean following close behind the advancing infantry and 'leap-frogging' batteries by sections to ensure that guns were always within range of the targets that might materialise during the advance.

During the night of 11th–12th March, the two brigades that were not taking part in the attack, 161 and 163 Infantry Brigades, pushed parties well forward into no-man's land a little to the north-east of the villages of Nabi Tari and Qule. These parties established a line of outposts to protect the infantry's forming-up points and start lines and the direct support batteries' positions, which had previously been reconnoitred by Colonel Dunbar and Captain Bailey, first as early as 20th February, then again on the morning of 11th March. Major Stanley later recalled:

> "As soon as darkness fell on 11th March, we started off to trek to the position for the morning's attack. This involved a detour past Yehudiye, through Wilhelma, across the railway, and into the foothills by the village of Et Tire, where the route turned to the north again. Then,following one of those irritating tracks which are so clear on the map but almost invisible on the ground, we reached our destination without misadventure. Having sent away the horses to wagon lines near Et Tire, all ranks lay down round the guns about midnight to get some sleep before the attack opened.
>
> Just before dawn on 12th March the infantry formed up for the attack. The first objectives were the village of Muzeira and the hills immediately to the east of it, which were held by the Turks. The intervening space was occupied by two very deep and steep wadis and the hamlet of Qule . . . Owing to the intention of surprise, no registering was possible and calculations for range and direction had all to be made from the not very reliable maps. Owing to the immense difficulties of the ground, the exact time when the infantry would be ready to assault could not be prearranged, so it was ordered that a signal should be sent to Major Stanley and the first round from B battery was to be a warning to the other batteries to open fire. All went well. The infantry – Londons and Bedfords – were seen to disappear into the wadis in the pale light and then to reappear scrambling up the steep

hillsides like lines of ants. Bang went the first gun, the shell burst beautifully on the top of the ridge, and the chorus joined in."

It does not seem as if B Battery's occupation by night was quite as simple a matter as Major Stanley suggests. Captain Bailey recorded his impression of the occupation and subsequent action as follows:

"All our batteries went forward into action in no man's land in the dark, to be in position by dawn to support the attack on the Muzeira Ridge at close range. I took A and C Batteries into action. Colonel Dunbar was taking B Battery in, as he had a special place north-east of Qule for them. When A and C were safely in action and teams away, I walked over to the right to find B Battery. They had found out that Dunbar's position was inaccessible owing to rocks, etc., and no alternative position had been reconnoitred. Dunbar left it to Stanley and myself to get the battery into action as best we could. We had, in the dark, to choose a position which was covered, and yet from which we could clear the crest at under two thousand yards. I finally chose a position where the crest was fairly level and pretty close in front and took the battery in with Stanley. Got back to the wagon lines at 1.0 a.m. and slept till 4.30 a.m.

Got up at 4.30 a.m. (*12th March*) and went up to battle headquarters just north-east of B Battery's position. As dawn broke we discovered that by good luck B Battery's position was perfect. They could clear the crest and were hidden, but I should think their flashes were probably visible from the top of Muzeira Ridge. The infantry advanced to Muzeira and we moved our battle headquarters there; no opposition to speak of. Moved the batteries forward and got some guns (*of A Battery*) right up on top of Muzeira Ridge by double teaming. Pushed straight on and captured Khirbet Bikerin, overlooking the Wadi Deir Ballut, on the further (northern) side of which stood the fortress of Majdal Yaba. The infantry collected in the wadi and stormed Majdal Yaba under cover of a bombardment, the heavies at Mulebbis joining in from the left. The bombardment finished with two minutes of smoke shell as a signal to the infantry to assault. It was a grand sight – the smoke shell bursting pure white with a stab of flame in the middle, giving the appearance of an old picture of the Peninsular Wars. The whole fortress of Majdal Yaba, standing up on a high rock, was wreathed in smoke. The infantry captured it and also Sheikh Es Din, a tomb and small mosque on a piece of high ground just to the north."

The day's objectives gained, Colonel Dunbar and Captain Bailey accompanied Brigadier-General Mudge, commanding 162 Infantry Brigade, around the new front-line positions, which followed the line of the Wadi Abu Lejja–Wadi Deir Ballut on the high ground about two thousand yards to the north-east. They organised defensive fire, which was not called upon, since the Turks showed no sign of counter-attacking, though they did shell Majdal Yaba heavily after it had fallen to the advancing Londons. Some idea of the mood following this complex but extremely successful operation can be judged from Captain Bailey's remarks:

"We camped for the night in a wadi half-way between Muzeira and Khirbet Dikerin with Headquarters 162 Infantry Brigade. We all had dinner together. A large mail arrived and everyone was in the best of form. It was just like a shooting lunch. The battle had been a most capital affair. We only lost one man and everything had gone exactly as planned."

Similar success accompanied 75th Division's advance on the right and in summing up the results of the actions on 11th–12th March 1918, the *Official History* reflects, in more measured tones, the elation expressed by Captain Bailey. In summary, it concluded that, "The line won was most favourable, with excellent covered positions for artillery". Success had been largely due to our preponderance in both field and heavy artillery; had there been anything approaching equality, the British field batteries would not have been able to move forward as they did, and the infantry would only have succeeded at vastly increased cost in casualties, compared with just over one hundred actually incurred by the three attacking brigades. Advantage in numbers of artillery was not all, however. Tactical handling, close co-operation with the infantry and huge effort on the part of all ranks (and their horses) were also instrumental in adding the day to the long list of achievements that constitutes '*Ubique*'.

There were no plans for immediate follow-up to the success of 12th March and units of 54th Division settled into a defensive routine on their new front. New ad-hoc artillery groups were formed covering the left and right sectors of the divisional frontage. Headquarters 270 Brigade added A/272 to its own three batteries and became No. 1 R.A. Group, responsible for the right sector. New positions for group headquarters and the batteries on the south bank of the Wadi Deir Ballut were reconnoitred on 13th March and occupied under cover of darkness on the night of 14th–15th. These positions posed particular difficulties. The north bank of the wadi, which was well inside our front line, was a cliff, two hundred feet high in places, marking the edge of the plateau across which future action would take place. The lack of suitable gun positions immediately north of the wadi led Colonel Dunbar to select the only possible area on the south bank – an interval in the cliffs where the ground, strewn with rocks and boulders, sloped much more gently southwards. The north bank would give cover from view and flash cover but was only three hundred yards away and presented serious crest-clearance problems; the guns would be on a forward slope but could gain some protection from the rocks. Detailed reconnaissance involved much "calculating and debating", according to Stanley, and it was decided that the guns should be placed as high as possible up the available slope. Then:

> "An hour or so after dark, the batteries moved in. A Battery were able to drive all their guns into place, but B Battery's position alongside them was impossible for horses and each gun had to be handled separately over the rocks by hand. There were fifty or more men on the ropes, many of which broke under the strain, causing broken shins and elbows. There was, however, a spice of novelty about it after years of digging in sand and mud . . . As digging was out of the question, 'sangars' of rocks took the place of gun-pits, and a new form of camouflage had to be adopted, since the limestone rocks showed big patches of white where they were not covered with flowers or moss. Every bivvy-tent and shelter had to be daubed with blotches of . . . whitewash made from crushed limestone."

Group headquarters moved into a high cave in the south bank of the wadi and lost no time in working out 'night lines' and defensive barrages, as well as planning for the eventual advance towards the obvious next objective, Kufr Qasim, which stood, readily visible from the O.P.s, on a ridge some three miles to the north. Turkish probing attacks occurred at intervals; all were successfully beaten off by the comprehensive system of defensive barrages, involving both field and heavy artillery. Of much more immediate threat to the batteries were the bombardments, known as 'hates', which the Turks put down at irregular intervals. They were usually by 5.9-in. howitzers, the shells of which burst on the surface of the rocky ground, adding lethal pieces of rock to their own splinters. Group headquarters were relatively safe in their cave, which seemed to attract quite a number of 'visitors' during these bombardments. Bombing from the air took place at intervals and air observation accounted for the accuracy of some of the shelling. Captain Bailey recorded that on one occasion during bombardment of the headquarters cave by 5.9s " . . . our wireless could pick up their signals and as we knew their code, we could tell exactly what corrections were given after every round, until a shell smashed our aerial". Bombardments were not all incoming, of course; each 'hate' led to a retaliatory 'strafe', and a great deal of effort was made, with some success, to locate the offending batteries and bring down effective counter-battery response from the heavy guns.

The German spring offensive on the Somme began on 21st March 1918 and had what the *Official History* describes as an "instantaneous effect" in the Palestine theatre. On 23rd March, Sir Edmund Allenby was ordered to send one of his British divisions to France. He selected 52nd Division, of XXI Corps, which sailed early in April after relief on the coastal plain to the immediate left of 54th Division by 7th Indian Division. In addition, a number of Indian cavalry regiments arrived in Palestine to replace Yeomanry regiments transferred to France, and Indian infantry battalions replaced some of the British battalions in the 10th, 53rd, 60th and 75th Divisions. Late in April, 3rd Indian Division arrived to replace 74th Division in XX Corps. It was an indicator that 54th Division was earmarked as the next division to go to France that it was not 'diluted' by Indian troops.

Despite these changes in his order of battle, and the need to accustom the newly arrived Indian units to their new theatre, General Allenby did not abandon his plan to continue the advance by a bold operation on XXI Corps' front. The 54th and 75th Division would open a significant gap in the Turkish line in the general area of the road–rail junctions at Qalqilye and the Australian Mounted Division would pass through to move swiftly on the Turkish Eighth Army's headquarters at the important junction of Tul Karm, some fifteen miles north of the present line. These operations began on 9th April, when 75th Division undertook the first

Plate 61   *Members of B/270 sightseeing in Cairo, June 1918. The prolonged lull in operations in the summer of 1918 allowed officers and men to be sent on leave in quite large numbers, though leave to England was out of the question.*
(Regimental Collection)

phase of the planned four-phase attack. The left flank of the attack was readily visible from 270 Brigade's O.P.s and they were able to support the bitterly contested battle for the prominent feature 'Three Bushes Hill' by enfilade fire. The advance was, on this occasion, against German troops, who put up determined resistance combined with swift counter-attacks against any positions they lost. By the end of the second day's fighting in what was later unofficially termed the 'Action of Berukin', 75th Division had not yet gained all its objectives. Despite this set-back, during the afternoon of 10th April orders came in to 270 Brigade for the second phase, the key features of which were the move of 54th Division northwards through the high ground at Kufr Qasim to Hable, and then in a wide right hook to face the railway and road between Jaljulye and Qalqilye. This would form the start line for the third phase, the capture of Jaljulye and Qalqilye, from which would be launched the final advance north-westwards to 'roll up' from the flank the Turkish trenches facing 7th Indian Division. Captain Bailey issued the brigade operation order for the advance on Kufr Qasim on 13th April, followed on 14th April by orders for the support of a preliminary advance by 1st/4th Northants of 162 Infantry Brigade. The Northants' 'show' was cancelled at the last minute and on the morning of 15th April Bailey recorded, "All operations against Kufr Qasim, etc. are cancelled, owing, it is believed, to the news from France". Stanley attributed the abandoning of these operations to the capture, probably as early as 9th April, of documents revealing the overall plan and the *Official History* confirms that this was indeed the case. But the reasons for the Turkish success were more complex, not least among them being "the defence and determination in counter-offensive of the two German battalions, with their numerous machine-guns and trench mortars, and the support of their own artillery".

Another Lull, April–June 1918

It was now clear that there would be no further general advance for some time, and that the British line must be stabilised and defended exactly where it had 'run out of steam' in mid-   [79]

April. New defensive fire schemes for the 54th Division's sector were worked out and repeat-edly revised over the coming months. In a redistribution of the fire units of No. 1 Group, responsible for 'Right Section' of the sector, B and C Batteries were moved almost at once, B from their hard-won position on the wadi bank to an area just south of Khirbet Dikerim and C still in the wadi but some four hundred yards 'upstream' to the south-east. Eventually a whole series of available positions were identified, reconnoitred and surveyed, and batteries moved between them from time to time, partly to conform to the latest defensive fire scheme, partly to confuse the Turkish counter-bombardment organisation, and partly, it must be admitted, to help relieve the stagnation that almost inevitably descends on troops manning static positions for any length of time. Firing was infrequent and restricted to necessary regis-tration of new targets and retaliatory 'strafes' following Turkish bombardments. Early in May a heavy trench mortar battery joined No.1 Group and defensive fire plans were further revised to incorporate this addition to the group's firepower.

The continuing stability of the front, combined with the detailed and practised defensive fire plans, enabled guns to be 'rested' for short periods for the first time since before the Third Battle of Gaza. A suitable camp, under the close supervision of H.Q.R.A. 54th Division, was established at Rantye and batteries went there for two weeks each. Rest was hardly the right description for the week of "marching, mounting guards, presenting arms, burnishing har-ness and ceremonial of all kinds" (Stanley) that filled the first week of B Battery's fortnight out of the line, but it was followed by worse. The second week consisted of "even more violent exercises, followed by every kind of inspection by everyone with any excuse to inspect – from the sanitary expert to the Corps Artillery Commander". The culmination of the two weeks was a march-past before C.R.A. 54th Division, a real challenge, since only Major Stanley had ever taken part in a march-past before. The event went off "exceedingly well", no doubt after much practice, but by the time the next battery came out of the line the description 'Rest' had been altered to 'Going into Reserve'!

By the middle of May 1918, Headquarters 270 Brigade/No. 1 R.A. Group was due for a period 'in reserve' and Captain Bailey was very busy making arrangements for handover. He assembled a huge dossier relating to the defence schemes but the Q(Ops) side of the work did not go so well. "The batteries gave a lot of trouble by making a desperate mess of ammuni-tion returns", he recorded on 16th May – a complaint that has endured down the years! The brigade also contrived to increase the number of horses on strength by exchanging mules for horses with the heavy trench mortar battery and the machine-gun company attached to 162 Infantry Brigade. Mules are not shown on the war establishment for field artillery brigades in the Egypt–Palestine theatre but were issued in lieu of horses, though not, generally, for gun- or ammunition wagon draught. The love-hate relationship that seems always to exist between drivers who are used to horses but have to make do with mules, against everybody's better judgement, is apparent in contemporary records of 270 Brigade, perhaps with just a little more love, based on the hardiness of the beasts, than hate. Whether the practice of horse–mule exchange had any official backing, and how long the brigade managed to keep the extra horses, is unfortunately not on record.

If proof were needed that the front was still active, it came on the night of 20th–21st May – the night before Headquarters 270 Brigade was due to hand over command of No. 1 Group and responsibility for the artillery defence of Right Section to Headquarters 272 Brigade. The Turks attacked and "there was a battle all night", according to Captain Bailey, who seems to have adopted a rather relaxed attitude in advance. He "conducted operations very comfortably, lying in bed with a candle, a fighting map and a telephone, calling out the latest news to Dunbar, whose bivvy is next door". That done, the headquarters moved from Khirbet Dikerim into billets in Mulebbis, rather than to the divisional artillery camp at Rantye. It was evidently planned that Headquarters 270 Brigade would return to the line in command of No. 2 Group/Left Section, for the same day Captain Bailey visited the existing headquarters, 271 Brigade, for briefing and on 22nd May he spent a large part of the day visiting the battery positions in the orchards to the north and north-east of Mulebbis and getting to know the ground.

As things turned out, neither Colonel Dunbar nor Captain Bailey would return to the line with 270 Brigade. Orders arrived on 23rd May that Colonel Dunbar was to transfer to com-mand of 53 Brigade, R.F.A., which was in process of formation in 3rd (Lahore) Division. Advance warning of the commanding officer's posting had apparently reached 270 Brigade some time previously and Dunbar had invited Bailey to go with him as adjutant. Bailey had agreed, principally on the ground of his dislike for H.Q.R.A. 54th Division, which, he recorded, he "could not stick much longer". Bailey's professionalism and grasp of detail is apparent from his diary, which includes as appendices many of the operation orders and defensive schemes that he prepared. He admitted, however, that he had not been at all popular with the staff at 'division' since they had discovered that he kept pinned to the wall in Headquarters 270 Brigade a substantial piece of paper headed 'The Sins of the Staff Captain', on which he entered details of all the mistakes for which S.C.R.A. 54th Division was responsible and to which Adjutant 270 Brigade had supplied corrections! Colonel Dunbar was due to leave on the day following receipt of his posting order, so commanding officer and adjutant went at once to H.Q.R.A. to negotiate the release of the two of them at the same time. They failed, but the C.R.A. did agree that Bailey could follow one month later, after 'working in' the new adjutant. However, on 24th May Bailey took *Rex* to Mulebbis racecourse for a training gallop. While galloping very fast, *Rex* caught both forelegs in some wire and fell, and Bailey, who was unconscious for an hour, but turned out not to have any bones broken, was evacuated to hospital with concussion. The last diary entry covering his service with 270 Brigade remarks, wryly, "So the Colonel and the Adjutant *did* leave on the same day!"

Lieutenant-Colonel F.G.T. Deshon arrived at once to take command of 270 Brigade. At almost the same time Major V. E. Pringle handed over command of C/270 to Major G. Kinloch but the battery commanders of A and B Batteries, Major Geoffrey Lawrence and Major F.E.C. Stanley, soldiered on; indeed both would see the war out with the brigade.

Warned for Service in France, June 1918

Early in June, Headquarters 270 Brigade went back into the line and took command of No. 2 Group, but June was anything but a stable month. On 11th June Colonel Deshon was evacuated sick. Then, between 20th–26th the whole brigade was withdrawn to reserve and orders were received to reorganise to War Establishment Part VII A and prepare to move overseas. It very soon became clear that 54th Division had been ordered to France and there ensued a complex administrative nightmare. The new war establishment required all 'rear link' signallers to leave the brigade and remuster in the Signal Service of the Royal Engineers; they duly left on 26th June. No guns, wagons or other heavy equipment were to be taken to France, so they were all transferred to other units or to store, together, of course, with the equipment of the other two brigades of the divisional artillery. The first indication that all this hard work had been for nothing came as early as 27th June, when orders were received suspending the change in War Establishment. On 3rd July it was confirmed that 54th Division was not to go to France and would revert to command of XXI Corps. It took a further ten days for the brigade headquarters signallers, who fortunately had not yet joined the Sappers, to return, together with their equipment; for guns and wagons – not those originally handed in – to be drawn, and for the wagons to be filled with first-line ammunition; for the 'new' guns to be handed back and replaced by the 'original' guns – much to every No. 1's relief, no doubt; and for all the necessary draught and riding horses and mules to be taken on strength. On 13th July 270 Brigade was very nearly complete and fit for war again, lacking only a few animals, and on 16th July the whole of the 54th Divisional Artillery marched to a reserve area at Ibn Ibrak, a few miles east of Jaffa, to await events.

B Battery in the Jordan Valley, August 1918

Within a few days, B/270 was detached from the brigade and joined an ad-hoc group formed from all units of 54th Divisional Artillery (H.Q. 272 Brigade, A/272, B/270, B/271 and a section of 54th Divisional Ammunition Column) in order to relieve the Royal Horse Artillery batteries of the Desert Mounted Corps in the Jordan Valley. Throughout the First World War, mounted formations were very much undergunned compared with infantry formations, having only one battery of R.H.A. to each mounted brigade, while three batteries normally supported an infantry brigade. Once in a relatively static position, as the Desert Mounted Corps had been for some months, the workload on the Gunners mounted and Stanley described the batteries that the ad-hoc group were due to relieve as "much depleted in numbers and efficiency through sickness, casualties and overwork".

Plate 62 *A wagon of B Battery, 270 Brigade moving to detached duty in the Jordan Valley, August 1918. The battery was to form part of a 'scratch' brigade consisting of one battery from each of the brigades of the 54th Divisional Artillery. B Battery returned to 270 Brigade in time for XXI Corps' renewed advance in mid-September 1918.*
(Regimental Collection)

The long trek to the Jordan valley began on 1st August 1918 and led through some very difficult country, with halts at Surafend, Latron, Enab and on the outskirts of Jerusalem, to a "loathsome bivouac area at Talat ed Dumm", close to Headquarters Desert Mounted Corps. It took a further two days to reach the battery's first gun position, on the edge of the Wadi Auja (not to be confused with the river of the same name near Jaffa), which was occupied by night. Then, only two days later, the battery was ordered to move a mile further west to replace a different outgoing battery. This position was "even better placed than the first and each gun and its detachment lived in a bower of green on the edge of the stream", with the O.P. about a mile forward in the trenches on "a rocky sun-blistered spot called Abu Tillul, the scene of much fighting", now manned by the Australian Light Horse. The six 18-pdrs. of B/270 took the place of two 4-gun 13-pdr. batteries, and orders were that there was to be as little shooting as possible, except in emergency, in order to avoid giving away the fact that there had been a change. However, "two sections of 60-pdrs., one on the right and one on the left, kept up the illusion of strength, fired a great deal, and provoked a lot of retaliation". It was as a result of one of these retaliatory 'hates' that the battery's regard for mules increased markedly. Two men had been wounded, and presumably attended to at once, but it was not until the next 'stables' parade that one mule was found to have "a narrow splinter of shell about seven inches long sticking out of its forehead like the horn of a unicorn", apparently without feeling any ill effects. Sickness was a far greater problem than enemy action, however, and affected especially "the younger men and the older horses". During the four-week spell in the Jordan Valley, 36 men were evacuated to hospital with malaria, and although many of them returned later, nothing was done to provide immediate reinforcements.

At length, the whole group was withdrawn without replacement and began the difficult journey back to rejoin 54th Division, which was once more in the line near Majdal Yaba. The rigours of the trek were relieved part-way by a day spent in bivouac outside Jerusalem, which allowed all ranks to visit the city. A further four night marches and the group was back in the 54th Divisional area with a few days in which to recover before going into the line. A mild form of fever, perhaps in reaction to the change in climate and conditions, now struck and B/270 lost a further 58 men to hospital in two days. It was accordingly with a strength of less than half their establishment that the battery rejoined 270 Brigade on 11th September.

Armageddon and after, September–October 1918

Meanwhile, during the nights of 29th–30th and 30th–31st August, Headquarters 270 Brigade had taken over once more as Headquarters No. 1 R.A. Group and, with A/270, B/272, C/270 and a battery of 4-in. trench mortars under command, had relieved 4 Brigade, R.F.A. of 3rd Indian Division in the line that they had left in June, running eastwards from Majdal Yaba. In the continuing absence of Colonel Deshon, Lieutenant-Colonel D. B. Stewart had been posted to command 270 Brigade on 7th July and it was under his command that the brigade would fight through the final operations in Palestine.

August 1918 turned out to be a busy month, as preparations were made for the expected advance and action was taken to distract or confuse the Turks. The British front line had now been occupied for more than four months and considerable effort had been made over this time to develop the potential of the artillery resources in various situations. When they reoccupied the line as Headquarters No. 1 Group, this time on the left of the 54th Division front, 270 Brigade took over 27 ready-surveyed and prepared positions for occupation as necessary by batteries under command. Of these, twelve were 'first line' positions for day-to-day use, seven were 'withdrawn' positions to be occupied if the line were pushed back, and eight were 'offensive' positions, sited well forward to allow maximum use of the relatively short range of the 18-pdrs. and 4.5-in. howitzers in the opening stages of an advance. Each of the batteries permanently under command of No. 1 Group was allocated two first line, two withdrawn and two offensive positions, the second, in each case, being for use as an alternative position should counter-battery fire force withdrawal from the first position. Positions were also allocated to three 'reinforcing' batteries that were in reserve but would hasten back to the line in the event of a Turkish attack. All these positions were linked by an extensive, permanent network of telephone lines. A defence scheme, consisting largely of pre-planned barrages, had, of course, been worked out and all necessary target information was obtained by registration and kept up-to-date by further registration shoots during the periods of 'artillery activity' which were designated by H.Q.R.A. XXI Corps. During 'artillery activity', additional batteries that would otherwise have been unemployed, or were particularly suitable for certain tasks, moved into No. 1 Group's area and came under temporary command. During August there were visits by sections of 13 and 17 Mountain Batteries and by the 'Hun Battery', a collection of captured enemy guns, all of German manufacture, which travelled along the front pausing at intervals to fire captured ammunition back at its original owners.

General Allenby had given his three corps commanders an indication of his plans for the resumption of the advance on 1st August. Three weeks later he gave them an outline of a much bolder scheme, for which detailed instructions were issued on 9th September. On the coastal plain, XXI Corps (3rd and 7th Indian Divisions, 54th and 75th Divisions, reinforced by 60th Division detached from XX Corps, and 5 Australian Light Horse Brigade) would attack northwards, and after capturing the Turkish trench systems, which in places were more than five miles in depth, would turn north-eastwards to drive the enemy from the line Tul Karm–Sebustiye (the main west–east route to the strategic centre, Nablus). The Desert Mounted Corps would meanwhile make a wide sweep northwards and then eastwards, to cut the reinforcement routes from the north and prevent the enemy from retreating, while XX Corps advanced directly on Nablus from the south. An overwhelming weight of artillery – nearly four hundred guns, including eighteen medium and heavy batteries – was allotted to XXI Corps' fifteen mile front. The ammunition supply was generous, too, with 1,000 rounds available for each 18-pdr. and 800 rounds for each 4.5-in. howitzer. Considerable resources were devoted to concealment of the moves of large numbers of troops in readiness for the attack; a deception plan was put into force; and plans were made for the Royal Air Force to strike Turkish command and control centres as the attack began.

On the right of the XXI Corps front, 54th Division with under command the brigade-sized French *Détachement Français de Palestine et de Syrie* (D.F.P.S.) had the shortest distance to advance, for they were at the 'hinge end' of a fifteen-mile-wide door that was to be burst open. However, they faced the greatest depth and complexity of the Turkish defences and much the most difficult country. From their start line, which extended some six miles from Ras el Ain on the left (west) to Ra-fat on the right, they would wheel the whole front through nearly ninety degrees to face due east on the approximate line Khirbet Kefar Thilth–Ra-fat and then push forward to secure Bidya. The artillery plan is admirably described in the *Official History*:

"There was to be no preliminary bombardment. The opening of fire by the artillery, trench mortars and machine-guns at 4.30 a.m. was to be the signal for the infantry to advance. The time had been selected so that there should be moonlight followed by thirty-five minutes of darkness before the first signs of dawn; this period was to be used for the deployment upon lines previously taped, in order to ensure that the troops formed up at right angles to the direction of their advance. The heavy artillery was to be devoted mainly to counter-battery work, certain guns and howitzers being employed to shell headquarters and telephone exchanges beyond the range of field artillery, and also, if available, points holding up the infantry. The field artillery was to bombard the enemy's front line until the arrival of the infantry. Then the 18-pdrs. and R.H.A. batteries were to lift and form a creeping barrage in front of the advancing infantry up to their extreme range, while the 4.5-in. howitzers fired on important points beyond the barrage . . ."

During the night of 11th–12th September B/270 moved back under command of 270 Brigade/No.1 R.A. Group, occupying a position alongside A/270 about a mile south-west of Majdal Yaba, with C/270 only a short distance away. For the next few days there was a definite increase in activity as new orders came through, plans were made and the count-down started to H-hour, which was fixed for 4.30 a.m. on 19th September. Left R.A. Group, under Headquarters 270 Brigade and consisting of A, B and C/270, C/271 and C/272, was in support of 161 Infantry Brigade on the left of 54th Division's advance. The first phase of the attack involved 4th and 5th Essex, who were to advance due north from their start line on the Haram Ridge, cross the Bureid Ridge and seize the high ground at Kufr Qasim – a total distance of some 3,500 yards. In the second phase, 6th and 7th Essex would move through and advance a further 1,800 yards to capture Kefar Bara, on the next ridge to the north.

After dark on 18th September, the batteries moved some 1,200 yards forward into 'offensive' positions only just behind our existing front line and a few hundred yards to the west of Majdal Yaba. The difficulty with which B Battery moved was described by Stanley:

"Twenty-five men returned to duty with the battery on 18th September. This, to some extent, saved the situation, but at the same time Lieutenant Woods, the senior of the two remaining subalterns, and a sergeant went sick. The net position was that there were only enough drivers for the lead and wheel horses; the centres went into action with gunners up and came out with only their good sense to guide them, for the gunners were required in the detachments."

Despite these difficulties, the batteries had completed their occupation by 9.00 p.m. and were able to get some rest before the next day's early start. Three hundred rounds per gun had already been dumped on the positions and camouflaged with straw and the guns each moved on to a marker which had, of course, been 'surveyed in'. The battery commanders sited their O.P.s on the railway north-west of Majdal Yaba, which here ran along an embankment, affording the best possible view eastwards at approximately right angles to the infantry advance some 3,500 yards away, or, as Stanley recorded, "a sufficient view of the first targets along the foothills".

A laconic entry in the brigade headquarters war diary which records that, on 19th September, "Operations commenced against the enemy at zero-hour – 04.30 – in accordance with 54th Division artillery plan" fails to convey the atmosphere of the last set-piece battle in the Palestine campaign. Stanley later recalled:

Plate 63   *R.S.M. W.G. Coles, of Watford. After several years of service as battery sergeant-major of 2nd Herts Battery, he was appointed regimental sergeant-major of 270 Brigade, R.F.A. in 1917 and served as such until demobilisation. With his comrades of 2nd Herts Battery, W.O.II J. Humphries and W.O.II G. F. Smith (see Plate 34), he was awarded the Territorial Force Efficiency Medal in 1920.*

(Regimental Collection)

"At 3.30 . . . after a final look-round, I tramped off in the dark to the O.P. on the railway, which I reached shortly before 4.30, as the first glimmer of dawn appeared. Lawrence was already in his O.P. fifty yards further along the bank. At 4.30 . . . the 383 guns of XXI Corps and those of two destroyers off the coast opened the bombardment. Owing to some trick of acoustics, as well as the length of the front, the noise was insignificant compared with our previous big battles, and even the bark of our own 18-pdrs. at the foot of Majdal Yaba seemed strangely muffled.

The particular role of B Battery was to fire smoke shells for the first hour or so, and create a screen in front of three commanding heights that afforded the enemy a fine view over the plain, changing to shrapnel and H.E. when this smoke should begin to be a hindrance to our own observers.

It was interesting to watch the effect of the smoke shells on the slopes of Sivri Tepe and Oglu Tepe, many of them ricochetting off the rocks and bursting in the air with a long trail of flame like fireworks. In the growing light it was pleasing to see that the still, damp air was holding the smoke in a long wall in front of these heights."

The leading assault battalions, 4th and 5th Essex, crossed the Bureid Ridge with no difficulty, shielded by the smoke, and moved down into the Wadi Raba having captured some seventy Turks. After pausing to regroup in the wadi, they moved on up the opposite bank and stormed Sangar Hill, immediately south of Kufr Qasim, killing or capturing all its defenders. Here, there was a further pause of fifteen minutes to allow the assaulting troops to regroup and the brigade machine-gun company to move up so that they could cover the next stage of the advance, from Sangar Hill across to slightly higher ground and on to the final objectives, Jevis Tepe on the left and the village of Kufr Qasim on the right.

By now the timed barrage programme had finished and the batteries were moving forward. The ground across which they had to advance was in large part visible from the very enemy positions which the supported battalions were attacking, and the batteries were shelled as they crossed the Wadi Raba and from then on were subject to both shelling and machine-gun fire. Major Stanley reached the Wadi Qasim close to the areas in which A and B Batteries were to deploy:

"In the wadi I met a company of Londons, old friends of Bald Hill days, who were lying amongst the rocks, sheltering from the considerable hail of machine-gun bullets that was coming over . . . From them I learned that things were not going too easily, and that the Turk was giving great trouble with machine-gun fire from Jevis Tepe and Sivri Tepe just in front.

By this time the other two sections had come up and the whole battery was in action. With B.S.M. Hancock, Sergeant Bell and the rest of the battery staff, I scrambled up the steep side of the wadi and found a place from which a fair view could be obtained. From here we opened fire on the two Tepes, and, thanks to the close range, were able to hit very hard. Several heavy batteries were also turned on to them, so that half an hour later, when Lawrence, breathless, joined me at my O.P., opposition was broken and we could confine our attention to assisting the departure of the Turk, pursued by the triumphant men of Essex.

My O.P. . . . was quite the least useful and most exposed I ever had. Any attempt to stand up . . . was, when I first arrived, greeted with an extra fierce gust of machine-gun fire and shrapnel, though, luckily, most of the former went over our heads and into the Wadi Qasim behind, while the shrapnel all burst short, though near enough to be unpleasant. The battalion which I was particularly supporting had as their successive objectives the series of rocky conical bumps – they could hardly be called hills – which fringed the foothills; some were named on the map, most were not, and it was difficult to tell from our crouching position among the rocks which bump they were on, and which the Turk, especially as there was very little to be seen of the latter.

Before running away or being captured, the Turk had, as usual, sent over salvo after salvo with his guns, probably unobserved, all along the Wadi Qasim, and, looking back, it seemed to me that they were all over my battery and A, but the fact of having come into action further back than was originally intended saved them, and though the gun shields were well splashed with bullets and splinters there were no casualties."

It was for gallantry in these conditions that Corporal Runchman, signaller in Major Lawrence's O.P., was awarded the Distinguished Conduct Medal. It had not been possible to bring wire forward from the new battery position and signalling between O.P. and guns was by flag. Corporal Runchman stood "in the open under heavy shell, machine-gun and rifle fire . . . and thereby enabled his battery commander to be always in communication with the battery".

By about 2.00 p.m., 161 Infantry Brigade had secured all their objectives and 162 Infantry Brigade were moving through and turning to advance to the east. By the small hours of 20th September the 54th Division and D.F.P.S. had secured all their objectives. The *Official History*, while crediting them with success over the most difficult ground, says that "resistance was never really stout". This view is not borne out by the *Brief Record of the Advance of the E.E.F.*, which says that strong resistance was encountered by 161 Infantry Brigade at Qasim Wood and again at Sivri Tepe. The fact that the level of resistance can be minimised may owe a great deal to the part played by 54th Divisional Artillery and the medium and heavy batteries under command, who had in many cases, and certainly on 161 Infantry Brigade's front, literally 'shot the infantry on to their objectives'. For the Gunners of 54th Division the shooting war ended during the afternoon of 19th September – but on a suitable note of success, summed up in the war diary of 270 Brigade, "Our troops successful everywhere. Casualties nil in brigade".

Action on the XXI Corps front ceased with the capture of Nablus on 21st September but Desert Mounted Corps, exploiting to the north, and the force in the Jordan valley, east of Jericho, continued fighting for another four days. On 26th September, General Allenby gave orders for the next phase of the advance. The Desert Mounted Corps was to make for Damascus, while XXI Corps was to advance up the coast from the most northerly town so far in British hands – Acre – and occupy Beirut. The extremely difficult lines of communication would make supply of more than two divisions north of the Haifa–Acre area impossible. Accordingly, 7th Indian Division, which was already concentrating in Haifa, was ordered to head the advance, starting on 3rd October, followed by 54th Division.

Occupation Duties, Cairo Garrison and Demobilisation, November 1918–June 1919

On 21st September, 270 Brigade left their last battle positions near the Wadi Qasim and moved a short distance south-west to concentrate with the whole of 54th Divisional Artillery near Ras el Ain. Two days later, the artillery rejoined the division at Jaljulye and dispositions were made for the move north, 270 Brigade remaining in support of 161 Infantry Brigade and coming under command for the move, as a 'brigade group'. Operational and administrative orders were issued by Headquarters 161 Infantry Brigade on 28th September and the following day the brigade group column set out on the six-day trek to Haifa. Here, the whole division remained in bivouac, just east of the town, for nearly three weeks. It was evidently an unhealthy spot and officers and men began to go down with malaria and other diseases. On 25th October the trek northwards along the coast, some three weeks behind 7th Indian Division, was resumed. The brigade group reached Acre the same night and then continued over the 'Ladder of Tyre' (see *The Hertfordshire Yeomanry – An Illustrated History* for details of the opening of the road over the Ladder of Tyre), through the towns of Tyre and Sidon and on to Beirut, which they reached on 2nd November. (Sources vary by up to three days on the dates on which units of 54th Division reached Beirut. It seems most likely the three brigade groups were intentionally timed to arrive on three successive days.) At Beirut, according to Stanley:

> "We went into a mixture of camps and billets to the north of the town . . . A semi-triumphal entry was made, the division saluting the Corps Commander as it marched through. It was received with applause and tears of joy by the famished inhabitants who had, as usual, been starved and ill-treated by the Turks, and who were dying in hundreds of hunger and privation.
>
> No sooner had the troops settled down than malaria and pneumonia broke out with accumulated force, and in no time the limited accommodation of the field hospitals was overflowing with sick. There were a large number of deaths. In the batteries there were scarcely enough fit men to attend to the horses. B Battery was, as usual, the lucky one; both A and C suffered severely and buried a dozen or more officers and men in the cemetery on the edge of the famous pine woods . . ."

The armistice with Turkey was announced on 31st October during 54th Division's trek to Beirut, so it was as troops of the Army of Occupation, or nearly so, that 270 Brigade suffered

Plate 64   *Saddler-Corporal Parmenter of C/270 in Egypt, early 1919. He is wearing the ribbon of the 1914–15 Star, which was instituted in December 1918 to recognise service on the establishment of a unit in an overseas theatre of war between 5th August 1914 and 31st December 1915. It was, accordingly, for their service in France in November–December 1915, rather than for service in Egypt and Palestine, that members of 4th East Anglian Brigade received this award.*
(Regimental Collection)

more than twice as many casualties in two months as they had in their various actions over two years. (Seven members of the brigade are buried at Beirut, one at Haifa, and seven who died after evacuation to Egypt are buried at Alexandria; remarkably, only six deaths were attributable to enemy action. See *Hertfordshire Yeomanry and Artillery Roll of Honour*.)

After four trying weeks in their bivouac at Mar Rukos, near Beirut, 270 Brigade received the welcome news that they were to proceed with the rest of 54th Division down the lines of communication to Egypt, there to await demobilisation. An advance party left on 3rd December and the main body travelled in two groups, leaving Beirut on 9th and 10th December. Almost the whole of the journey was by sea – from Beirut to Kantara, now an important port on the Suez Canal. By 13th December the brigade had reassembled and was encamped with 54th Division at Helmieh, near Cairo. Here, according to Stanley:

". . . It looked as if they had only to celebrate a peaceful Christmas together and then go home as fast as demobilisation would let them (*but*) the first news that greeted the reassembled division was that they had five days to prepare for a march past the Commander-in-Chief in Cairo. For the infantry it was a small matter, but the shock was a dreadful one for battery commanders. The move had been made by sea to Kantara and thence by train; the only boats available and the appliances for loading at Beirut had been the worst imaginable. Consequently, many of the vehicles were damaged and the harness and steel-work were in an appalling state, added to which the poor horses, which never carried very much flesh, were looking their very worst in their winter coats, which there was no time to clip."

Fortunately, a large number of men who had gone sick towards the end of the campaign, and had been evacuated to base hospitals in Egypt, rejoined and with huge effort the brigade reached a creditable level of smartness before setting off on 19th December on what turned out to be their final parade and march as a unit. There were already signs of unrest in Cairo and the route through the city was clearly planned to impress the local population with a 'show of strength'. Stanley recorded:

". . . The route to the saluting base was planned to include the heart of the native quarter of the city, and the column slowly travelled miles of squalid but interesting streets that otherwise would never have been seen. The day passed without any unpleasant incident, and it was for all a memorable moment when, in Opera Square, we looked for a few seconds in the face of the man who had led us from victory to victory in the past eighteen months, but whom, many of us, in the Gunners at any rate, had never seen before."

By Christmas 1918, the brigade was in a "spotless and well ordered camp, with the 48 guns of the divisional artillery in line for the first time". Christmas itself was spent in "riotous enjoyment and in full confidence of an early return home".

[87]

It took some weeks for the machinery of demobilisation to come fully into operation. Early in March, however, guns and ammunition wagons were handed back to store and horses began to leave; by the middle of the month about one-third of the brigade had left for home. At this point, however, the whole demobilisation process was stopped by serious civil unrest throughout Egypt. There was widespread destruction, particularly to communications, and a number of Europeans were murdered. The country was divided for internal security purposes into districts, with a general officer in command of each, and camps, garrisons and the main towns were guarded and patrolled by troops. There was a widespread requirement for cavalry, of which there was almost none in Egypt, to act as mounted police and 54th Divisional Artillery was pressed into service as '54th Division R.A. Mounted Regiment', for whom the issue pick helve replaced the long mounted police baton. Parties from the regiment, which was for a time commanded by Major Stanley of 270 Brigade, were stationed throughout the Cairo area, and Stanley recalled that men of his own battery – B/270 – were in five different places, including the grandstand of Gezireh racecourse. By the end of April matters had quietened down and troops remaining in Egypt were reorganised as part of the Army of Occupation. The mounted regiment was dispersed and demobilisation recommenced early in May, to finish during June. Many former members of 270 Brigade actually went home for demobilisation directly from the ad-hoc internal security units into which they had been bundled by the exigencies of the rebellion (Stanley) but Headquarters 270 Brigade remained in being until the end of June, led, except for the last few days, by Captain H.A. Raffe, who had succeeded Captain Bailey as adjutant in July 1918.

Chapter 7

The Second and Third Line Batteries and the Depot, 1914–1919

2nd/4th East Anglian Brigade, 1914–1919

In accordance with a series of instructions issued between 31st August and 29th December 1914[1], Reserve batteries were raised with effect from 1st September 1914, at Hertford for 1st and 2nd Herts Batteries, and at Peterborough for 1st Northants Battery. The initial cadres were provided by the relatively small number of men who had been embodied in August and who were unsuitable for Imperial Service through age or medical category, or who had not volunteered. The batteries conformed to the war establishment of a Territorial field battery (four 15-pdr. B.L.C. guns) – five officers and 140 non-commissioned officers and men – shown in detail in Appendix 2. By 19th September, Hertfordshire Territorial Association was able to take note that, since their two Imperial Service batteries were up to strength in rank and file and lacking only two officers, recently joined recruits were now being posted to the Reserve batteries. As a result, the combined strengths of these batteries stood at six officers and 154 men and four officers and 126 men were needed to complete the establishment. A similar situation may be presumed to have obtained in Northamptonshire but, to date, no attempt had been made in either county to form a Reserve ammunition column, since the Imperial Service ammunition column was still not up to establishment and had not yet been accepted for service abroad.

From the point of view of numbers alone, the Reserve batteries had quite quickly become viable draft-finding units, but there is room for considerable doubt about the standards of training achieved in the early months in the face of total lack of guns and serious shortages of other equipment, and of horses. In mid-November 1914, Hertfordshire Territorial Association noted that all its Imperial Service units had been fully fitted out with clothing, supply of which remained an Association responsibility until well into the war, and that the Reserve units would now be priority recipients. In addition to clothing, the Associations were continuing to supply harness, and driving drill could be carried out with impressed civilian carts, providing they were of pole-, rather than shaft draught. Ingenuity, which was never in short supply, helped considerably in the training of signallers but the gunners must have had difficulty in suspending their disbelief if they were, indeed, forced to train on 'Quaker' guns (stout wooden poles lashed to handcarts, for example), which would give them the opportunity of learning 'positions in action' but, in the absence of any form of sights, little else. There is, unfortunately, no record of the guns issued to the Reserve batteries before November 1915, when they received the cast-off 15-pdr. B.L.C.s from the Imperial Service batteries. Only then could the Reserve batteries have made any realistic contribution to the Home Forces order of battle, though from the summer of 1915 they had, according to Becke (see Bibliography), four antique French 90-mm. guns between them, with twenty rounds each of rather suspect black-powder ammunition, which were to be used only in the event of invasion.

The authority under which the Reserve batteries had been raised provided, in fact, for the formation of Reserve *units* or, in Gunner terms, brigades. It is hardly surprising, however, given the difficulties outlined earlier, that in Hertfordshire and Northamptonshire the batteries were given priority and were not linked by a brigade headquarters or provided with an ammunition column for some three months. It seems probable that the Reserve brigade came into being only after orders were received in December 1914 for units of the Reserve, or 2nd, East Anglian Division to move to a concentration area around Peterborough. Major O.R. McMullen, who had retired from 1st Herts Battery in 1912 and returned to command Reserve [89]

Plate 65   *Major O.R. McMullen, who was first commissioned in 1st (Hertfordshire) Volunteer Battalion The Bedfordshire Regiment in 1893 and transferred to command of 1st Hertfordshire Battery on formation in 1908, retiring in 1912. He rejoined on the outbreak of war in 1914 and was promoted to the command of 2nd/4th East Anglian Brigade the following year. In May 1916 he moved to extra-regimental employment and for two years was in command of 351 Brigade, R.F.A. He was appointed C.M.G. in January 1918.*   (Regimental Collection)

1st Herts Battery on the outbreak of war, was selected to take command of 4th (Reserve) East Anglian Brigade, but he was not promoted to lieutenant-colonel until June 1915.

On 17th December 1914, Hertfordshire Territorial Association was informed that the first draft had already left the Reserve brigade. The departure of 35 non-commissioned officers and men from the Hertfordshire batteries and fifteen from Northamptonshire was a blow to the continuity of the build-up of the brigade, both in numbers and in the standard of training. Additionally, though, it set at a very early stage the precedent – no doubt deemed undesirable by all concerned – of the draft going to reinforce an 'alien' unit, in this case a Wessex brigade under orders for India. Complete records have not survived but it is clear from the brigade war diary and the later 'Digest of services . . .' (see Bibliography and Guide to Sources) that throughout the war large numbers of officers and men were drafted to units other than 1st/4th East Anglian Brigade and its successor units. The intention that the 2nd Line Territorial brigades should serve as a reservoir of trained manpower for reinforcement as necessary is illustrated by the instruction issued early in 1916[2] that units of 2nd Line Territorial Divisional Artillery should consist only of men who were medically fit for general service and over 18¾ years of age – the age at which they could be posted to active service abroad. As the arrangements for recruit training changed (see below) and the manpower situation deteriorated, especially in the spring of 1918, the likelihood that a recruit enlisting into a Territorial artillery unit would actually join the 1st Line of that unit decreased very significantly.

Early in 1915, 2nd East Anglian Division moved to a new area centred on Thetford, Norfolk. Here, the brigade and its constituent batteries dropped 'Reserve' from their titles and became 2nd/4th East Anglian Brigade with batteries designated 2nd/1st and 2nd/2nd Hertfordshire and 2nd/1st Northamptonshire and with 2nd/4th East Anglian Brigade Ammunition Column[3]. The division was not allocated a place in the numbered series of Territorial divisions until August 1915, when it became 69th Division.[4]

For three months from early August to mid-November 1915, 54th Divisional Artillery, which had not sailed for Gallipoli with its own division, was attached to 69th Division. It is not on record whether formal arrangements were made for the 2nd Line units to train on equipment belonging to the 1st Line units fortuitously encamped so close, but it seems hardly possible that the opportunities would have been ignored. There was a big influx of recruits in October and November 1915, all for foreign service, and the transfer in November 1915 of the

Plate 66   *B.Q.M.S. F.C. Jones of Watford, who had already received the Volunteer Long Service Medal for twenty years' service in the Volunteer Artillery when he joined 2nd Herts Battery as its first battery quartermaster-sergeant in 1908. He retired in 1912 but rejoined on the outbreak of war in 1914 and served for two years as battery quartermaster-sergeant of 2nd/2nd Herts Battery.*   (Regimental Collection)

15-pdr. B.L.C. guns from the 1st Line was accordingly to a full-strength brigade, able to make good use, at last, of the proper complement of guns and ammunition wagons. The 15-pdr. B.L.C. guns did not remain in service with 69th Divisional Artillery for long. On 17th January 1916, 2nd/4th East Anglian Brigade received twelve 18-pdr. guns and 36 ammunition wagons. However, in order to conserve stocks of 18-pdr. ammunition and use up remaining 15-pdr. stocks, it had already been ordered that firing practice would be carried out using the 15-pdr., though only 100 rounds per battery were made available.[5]

Under the renumbering scheme for Territorial field artillery brigades, which took effect in May 1916 (see Chapter 1), 2nd/4th East Anglian Brigade became CCCXLVIII (348) Brigade. The batteries were designated A, B and C following their original seniority, and still with only four guns each. Later in the year 348 Brigade was completely reorganised. In order to form two 6-gun batteries B/348 (originally 2nd/2nd Herts) was broken up on 10th November 1916 and distributed between A and C/348. Until 26th December 348 Brigade consisted of only two 6-gun batteries, which retained the letters A and C. Then 345 Brigade (originally 2nd/1st East Anglian) was broken up and two of its batteries transferred to 348 Brigade. A/345 (originally 2nd/1st Norfolk) became B/348 and D (Howitzer)/345 (originally 2nd/1st Suffolk) became D (Howitzer)/348. It is unfortunately not clear whether it was intended that the batteries' original links with their counties (A – Hertfordshire, B – Norfolk, C – Northamptonshire, D – Suffolk) should be maintained. This would have been extremely difficult, though, and it seems most likely that 348 Brigade took on a more general East Anglian character.

Towards the end of June 1916, 69th Division moved from Thetford to Harrogate, Yorkshire, where units spent the summer and early autumn under canvas. The conventional move into 'winter quarters' took place in the middle of October when the division went into billets in Harrogate, Catterick and Doncaster. At the end of April 1917 the division once more moved into camps for the summer. This date coincides with the beginning of the 'Digest of Services' of 348 Brigade which has survived at the Royal Artillery Institution, with the result that considerably more is known about the brigade from May 1917 until demobilisation.

On 1st May 1917 the strength of 348 Brigade stood at 31 officers, 981 other ranks and 556 horses – about two hundred men over establishment and 120 horses under. The overbearing of men was gradually eroded until the strength reached 45 officers, 655 other ranks and 483 horses on 1st December 1917. Similar figures are shown until July 1918, when the strength of   [91]

NORTHANTS RESERVE B... R.F.A. CHURCH PARADE .7.

Plate 67 *The very early days of 1st (Reserve) Northamptonshire Battery, October–November 1914. Recruits who have not yet been issued with uniform outnumber trained soldiers marching to church in Peterborough.*
(Regimental Collection)

other ranks increased to 750, the level maintained until the end of the war. The movements of drafts in and out of the brigade are not fully accounted for in the Digest of Services and the best judgement that can be made is that the brigade was being used to provide 'continuation training' for men who had passed through initial training but were not yet required, or possibly were not yet old enough, for service abroad. 'Postings out' are almost invariably back to Reserve Brigades, one of the functions of which was to hold trained men fit for service abroad and provide drafts for overseas as required. From November 1917 – there are no details of earlier drafts – the exchange of men was with a variety of Reserve Brigades, so that 348 Brigade may well have become 'East Anglian' in name only by the end of the war. The most likely answer is that a cadre of older non–commissioned officers with links to the former East Anglian brigades remained, in all probability near to despair at how 'their' batteries had been diluted beyond recognition.

The summer of 1917 was spent with the whole of 69th Divisional Artillery in Nottinghamshire, broken by a few days in July during which 348 Brigade moved by rail to practice camp on Salisbury Plain and returned the same way. A seven-day road march in mid-October took the brigade into winter quarters in Darlington, where they remained until the second week of April 1918. A Battery then proceeded by a seven-day march to Louth, in Lincolnshire, where the battery was attached to Humber Garrison Defences. The use of the battery to reinforce part of the East Coast fixed defences may have been as a result of the perceived increased threat of German raids or may have reflected the decrease in manpower in the fixed defences resulting from emergency drafts to France in the face of the Germans' success during their spring offensive. At the end of April the remaining batteries moved, partly by train and partly by road march, to Carburton Camp, near Doncaster, to spend another summer – the last, as things turned out – under canvas.

The summer of 1918 was remarkable for a two-day visit by G.O.C.-in-C. Home Forces to 69th Division, during which he inspected 348 Brigade, less A Battery, both in camp and during field training, and for the exchange, at last, of D Battery's 5-in. howitzers for 4.5-in. howitzers. The whole brigade assembled on Salisbury Plain for two weeks' practice camp during September. Then, as usual, early in October, came the move into billets for the winter. A Battery, still part of East Coast defences, moved to Grimsby, while the rest of the brigade marched the short distance into Doncaster. On 1st November 1918, the Digest of Services records the brigade strength of 37 officers, 715 other ranks and 515 horses and the receipt, ten days before the armistice with Germany, of orders for the brigade to be disbanded. Horses began to be posted away at once and all had left by early December, while the strength of all ranks was reduced from 750 in mid-November to less than one hundred at the end of December. Before the end of January the processes of disbandment were complete and 348 Brigade had left the order of battle of Home Forces.

3rd/4th East Anglian Brigade, No. 4 T.F. Artillery Training School and 4th Reserve Brigade, 1915–1919

A strict interpretation of the instructions for the raising of '2nd Reserve' units issued in November 1914[6] suggests that these units were only to be raised "when an I.S. unit has proceeded abroad . . . and is replaced at the War Station at home by its 1st Reserve unit". It is

Plate 68 *Territorial Gunners of an unidentified unit at gun drill with a French 90-mm. field gun. Introduced in the French Army in 1877, the gun fired an 18-pound shell to a maximum range of 7,500 yards. In 1915, a number of Territorial brigades, including 2nd/4th East Anglian Brigade, were issued with these outdated weapons for use in the event of enemy landings, but they had only twenty rounds per gun of very suspect ammunition. The guns were of some value for training, though, to units which had been using wooden dummies.* (From 'Kitchener's Army . . .')

clear, however, that 2nd Reserve (later 3rd Line) units were raised when I.S. units were still in England and the spirit of the instructions may well have been taken to include units that had been selected for service abroad, or even those that had volunteered, rather than simply those that had actually sailed. Supplementary instructions were issued on 25th March 1915.[7] These required '3rd Line Depots' for the Territorial Force to be raised in accordance with attached schedules, but unfortunately the schedules detailing units and their establishments have not survived. It does seem probable that they covered 3rd Line Depots supporting 1st Line units that had not yet left for service abroad.

The 3rd Line Depot supporting 4th East Anglian Brigade was formed at Hertford, as 3rd/4th East Anglian Brigade, early in March 1915. It first appears in the *Return of the Territorial Force at Home* for 15th March with an establishment of 292 all ranks, including eight officers and seventeen sergeants. The strength crept up from seven all ranks on 15th March to eighty on 24th May and after a huge influx of recruits, all for service abroad, to 225 on 7th June. By the next return, on 21st June, the establishment had been increased to 316 all ranks with eight officers and nineteen sergeants, but there were still only two officers and three sergeants on the strength. Arrangements existed for 2nd Line units to lend officers and instructional staff to 3rd Line units but 2nd/4th East Anglian Brigade was hardly in a position to help. The small staff of the brigade depot (see below) were on hand, though, and may be assumed to have played a full part. There were, in any case, severe limits to the training that could be given in a 3rd Line artillery unit. Instructions issued in April 1915[8] reminded 3rd Line units that their aim was "to train individuals thoroughly to take their place at the front in as short a time as possible" but had opened with a statement that "no field guns, . . . horses, saddlery or harness . . . can at present be supplied". All material and horses necessary for training drafts would, according to the instructions, "have to be supplied for the present from 2nd Line units or otherwise from commands". The same instructions included an outline syllabus for recruits training with 3rd Line artillery units:

"N.C.O.s and gunners must have a thorough knowledge of section gun drill of the equipment with which the unit for which it is to produce drafts is armed. As large a number as possible must be trained as layers.

[93]

The following number of trained specialists should always be maintained:-

6 Signallers
6 Telephonists ⎬ For each 1st Line battery for which
2 Cold shoers ⎭ it has to produce drafts

All N.C.O.s must be taught to ride.

All drivers must be trained to ride and drive and be thoroughly instructed in the care and management of horses."

Those concerned with putting these instructions into effect could have been excused from the feeling that they were being ordered to attempt the impossible. Pragmatically, they may have settled for doing what they could in the circumstances.

Relief was planned quite soon but took some time to materialise. It was announced on 25th May 1915[9] that five Territorial Force Artillery Training Schools were to be established and that each 3rd Line Depot would be affiliated to one of the schools, which would be capable of accommodating and training half the establishment of all its affiliated depots at one time. 'Rotation' of personnel through the schools would be arranged so that all personnel would attend. During June the locations of the schools were announced and the affiliations of depots to schools, which had been fixed provisionally in May, were confirmed.[10] The three East Anglian field artillery depots providing drafts to units armed with the 15-pdr. B.L.C. gun (3rd/1st, 3rd/2nd and 3rd/4th) were affiliated to No. 4 T.F. Artillery Training School at High Wycombe. In July 1915 an establishment of horses was fixed for artillery 3rd Line Depots.[11] Field artillery depots were entitled to ten riding horses and fifty light draught horses "in excess of any issued to the different Artillery Training Schools". The horses were for training purposes only and were to be selected as far as possible "from those which are not suitable or ready for service overseas". There is evidence that 3rd/4th East Anglian Brigade at Hertford received their first horses towards the end of June 1915 but the build-up towards complete establishment is not recorded.

Early in October 1915 a syllabus was issued detailing the number of hours to be spent daily on key subjects over a period of twelve weeks in order to bring recruits to the necessary standard for drafting overseas.[12] The responsibility for training in accordance with the syllabus did not remain with 3rd Line units for long, however, for on 12th November 1915 they were ordered to concentrate at their affiliated schools.[13] By 20th December, 3rd/4th East Anglian Brigade, then with a strength of 459 all ranks against an establishment of 288, had moved to High Wycombe. They were instructed to take with them "all their horses, harness, saddlery, guns, carriages and other training equipment" but there is no indication that any guns had been issued. For the next eight months 3rd/4th East Anglian Brigade remained in being as a holding and drafting unit while No. 4 T.F. Artillery Training School provided the full range of instructional facilities and ran the necessary courses for recruits, specialists and potential non-commissioned officers. The increased availability of guns in the first six months of 1916, as the 18-pdr. replaced the 15-pdr. B.L.C. in 2nd Line units and eventually reached the schools, would have greatly eased the task of training gunners to the necessary standards.

The final step in the development of the training, holding and drafting procedures for recruits to Territorial field artillery units was taken in August 1916,[14] when 3rd Line units were absorbed by their affiliated schools, which were then reconstituted as fully fledged brigades with a permanent cadre of instructional and administrative staff and an establishment of personnel 'attached for drafting', who could be recruits under training, trained soldiers awaiting drafting or soldiers returned from abroad awaiting reposting. No. 4 T.F. Artillery Training School became 4th Reserve Brigade, R.F.A.(T.) and was established with headquarters and two batteries. A permanent cadre of just under two hundred all ranks were hosts to a floating population of trainees and others that could reach nine hundred. The direct connection between the Hertfordshire and Northamptonshire batteries and their own 3rd Line training and draft-finding unit thus ceased but the 1st and 2nd Line brigades continued to look principally to 4th Reserve Brigade for the provision of drafts and as the holding unit to which officers and men returned from abroad to await reposting or release.

4th Provisional Battery; 1206 (East Anglian) Battery, R.F.A.

It is clear from Hertfordshire Territorial Association records that there were "Detachments of R.F.A. with Provisional Units" as early as August 1915. It may accordingly be assumed that officers and men who were available only for Home Service (see Chapter 1) were removed from 1st/4th and 2nd/4th East Anglian Brigades and attached to an embryo Provisional Battery, though the battery is not detailed. An attractive assumption, based on information that becomes available later in the war, is that all four East Anglian brigades despatched their Home Service personnel to 4th Provisional Battery. This battery was raised within 4 Provisional Brigade to a War Establishment based on four 15-pdr. B.L.C. guns[15] and almost identical to that shown in Table 1 of Appendix 2. On deployment, 4 Provisional Brigade (46th, 47th, 48th and 49th Provisional Battalions) moved to counter-invasion stations on the north-east coast of Norfolk, with its field battery located a short distance inland, and in the centre of the brigade frontage, at North Walsham.

The brigade was still deployed in the same area when, on 1st January 1917,[16] it was redesignated 224 Infantry Brigade and its constituent battalions became 23rd Cheshire, 23rd Royal Welsh Fusiliers, 4th Monmouth and 14th South Lancashire, respectively. Reconstitution of 4th Provisional Battery resulted in 1206 (East Anglian) Battery, R.F.A. and since it is clear that the 'East Anglian' designation had nothing to do with the location of the battery itself, the assumption that it was composed of men from the East Anglian Divisional Artillery suggests itself. The battery continued to serve at North Walsham in support of 224 Infantry Brigade (224 Mixed Brigade from September 1917) until the end of the war. The establishment of 1206 Battery, which apparently did not move to the more usual 6-gun establishment, was 236 all ranks throughout 1917–18 – considerably more than a 4-gun 18-pdr. battery and possibly indicating that in the absence of any divisional ammunition column the battery held as an increment the equivalent of a section of a brigade ammunition column. Demobilisation followed swiftly upon the cessation of hostilities and 1206 Battery was disbanded in January 1919.

4th East Anglian Brigade Depot

Instructions for the formation of 'Territorial Force Depots' on mobilisation were issued in the form of an additional appendix to *Territorial Force Regulations* in July 1914.[17] Depots were to be formed "either for a single unit or for a group of units, for the purpose of attesting, medically examining, clothing and equipping recruits and despatching them to units". Recruits were not expected to remain at depots for more than 48 hours, since all their training would take place with their units at war stations. The establishment for T.F. Depots was accordingly set initially at "not more than one officer and one non-commissioned officer per unit affiliated" but was changed, no doubt in the light of experience, in November 1914 so that a field artillery brigade depot consisted of one officer, one sergeant, one corporal and four rank and file.

Following the raising of '3rd Line Depots' (see above) there was, inevitably, confusion between the two 'Depots' and instructions were issued in April 1915[18] for the original T.F. Depots to be redesignated 'Administrative Centres' and for the personnel to be permanently posted to each centre, rather than detached from affiliated units. Administrative Centres were to be commanded by an officer not below the rank of captain and were to be "independent of and outside the establishment of the 3rd Line Depot". Further instructions, issued in August 1915,[19] increased the duties of the Administrative Centres in relation to sick and wounded personnel and those temporarily released to civil employment. To undertake the extra duties, Administrative Centres were permitted to hold additional Home Service personnel up to fifty per cent of establishment. By March 1916, largely as a result of the introduction of conscription, the work-load on Administrative Centres had considerably decreased and Officers-in-Charge of Territorial Force Records, who were ultimately responsible for the proper functioning of Administrative Centres, were directed to consult Territorial Force Associations with a view to reducing the number by grouping the centres of various units.[20] The action taken as a result of these consultations was promulgated at the end of July 1916, when Administrative Centres reverted to the title 'Territorial Force Depot'.[21] Establishments for each depot were issued at the end of October 1916.[22] The various arms of the service gradually withdrew from the grouped T.F. Depots as their administrative and training arrangements were increasingly centralised. In the case of artillery units, this took place in February 1917, when the Territorial R.F.A. and R.G.A. depots were concentrated as T.F. sections of the Regular R.F.A. and R.G.A. depots in each command.[23]

Little is known about the depot formed by 4th East Anglian Brigade on mobilisation; indeed shortage of suitable personnel, especially officers, and the conflicting demands of Reserve 4th East Anglian Brigade, which was in process of formation at the same time and in the same place, may have delayed the opening of the depot. Its functions could relatively easily have been carried out by the Reserve batteries themselves, or possibly by just one of them – Reserve 1st Herts – which may have set men aside for the purpose. According to Griffith (see Bibliography), 'Major' A.K. Lofts was O.C. Depot, but Lofts was not commissioned into Reserve 1st Herts Battery until 27th October 1914 and it seems most likely that his appointment would have started at the time the Reserve batteries left Hertford in December 1914. Indeed, the depot is not listed in the *Return of the Territorial Force at Home* until January 1915. Apparently in accordance with the instructions that officers commanding Administrative Centres were not to be below the rank of captain, Lofts was promoted to the acting rank of captain, but not until October 1915, by which time the establishment had increased to one officer, one sergeant and nine rank and file – the standard establishment for a number of Administrative Centres, including those for field artillery. As a result of the consultations between Officers-in-Charge of T.F. Records and Hertfordshire Territorial Association that had taken place in March–April 1916, it was evidently agreed that a single Territorial Force Depot at Hertford could meet the requirements of the Hertfordshire Yeomanry, 4th East Anglian Brigade, R.F.A. and the Hertfordshire Regiment, and such a depot was brought into being during August 1916. The establishment of T.F. Depot, Hertford provided for only two officers but for one sergeant, one corporal and one private (or equivalent) from the Yeomanry, R.F.A. and infantry. This arrangement held until the R.F.A. component was withdrawn when all the East Anglian brigades came under the administration of No. 4 R.F.A. Depot at Woolwich in February 1917 and the idea of each brigade having its own depot within its recruiting area was abandoned.

NOTES:
1. A.C.I.s 310/Aug. 1914, 26 and 198/Oct. 1914, 271/Nov. 1914 and 266/Dec. 1914 and Army Order 399/1914
2. A.C.I. 96/1916
3. A.C.I. 258/Jan. 1915
4. A.C.I. 89/Aug. 1915
5. A.C.I. 115/Dec. 1915
6. A.C.I. 271/Nov. 1914 (superseded by A.C.I. 266/Dec. 1914)
7. A.C.I. 243/Mar. 1915
8. A.C.I. 195/Apr. 1915
9. A.C.I. 212/May 1915
10. A.C.I.s 122 and 213/June 1915
11. A.C.I. 175/July 1915
12. A.C.I. 81/Oct. 1915
13. A.C.I. 129/Nov. 1915
14. A.C.I. 1588/1916
15. *War Establishments, Part X – A Provisional Brigade* dated 1st July 1915, issued with Army Order 314/1915
16. A.C.I. 2364/1916
17. Army Order 226/1914
18. A.C.I. 146/Apr. 1915
19. A.C.I. 32/Aug. 1915
20. A.C.I. 648/1916
21. A.C.I. 1496/1916
22. A.C.I. 2060/1916
23. A.C.I. 347/1917

Epilogue – Last Post and Reveille

As has been shown, it was the fate of 270 Brigade to be broken up in Egypt and for officers and men to be sent home in small parties for demobilisation and release to civilian life. Major Stanley captured the effect of this misfortune when he recorded:

> "The official return of the battery took place in the early autumn of 1919, when that unrecognisable entity 'the Cadre', consisting of two men and a stationery box, commanded by a Canadian officer who had never served in the battery, arrived unheralded and unwanted in Peterborough, where the battery had mobilised over five years before."

A similar unceremonious dumping of records must have taken place in Hertfordshire. There were no marches through the battery areas, no civic welcomes, not even a note in the local newspapers. The war had now been over for several months and, with a widespread influenza epidemic and uncertain prospects for the economy, few were interested in the batteries' survival or future.

It had been the lot of the Hertfordshire batteries and of their comrades from Northamptonshire and Suffolk to serve in the 'shooting war' for less than two years, and in a theatre of war that was in most people's minds subsidiary to France and Flanders, if not actually a side-show. The officers and men of 270 Brigade were spared the horrors and the undoubtedly higher casualty rate of the Western Front but they nevertheless contended with great hardship and huge difficulties as they fought northwards through Gaza and into Palestine, and emerged victorious to occupy what is now Lebanon. In *The Forgotten Fronts* . . . Sir Martin Farndale ascribes Allenby's victories in part to the "morale, spirit and endurance of . . . men . . . (*who*) were a long way from home and suffered in appalling conditions of heat, rain and cold, frequently short of food, water and shelter" and goes on to pay tribute to the Gunners of the Egyptian Expeditionary Force:

> "... Almost to a man they were either Territorials or young men of the Empire who had had to learn the hard way. In truth the nature of the fighting gave them time to learn, but the complexity of handling artillery in rough going while manoeuvring and then at short notice concentrating fire rapidly called for a high degree of skill in command, communications and survey. This was at a time when these were not easy to achieve. Radio was rare, telephone line was never sufficient, success only came at close range, but somehow they always got there. Great credit is also due to those in the resupply organisation for achieving near miracles in getting the ammunition to the batteries. The guns . . . of the divisional artillery were the backbone of it all. Without them nothing would have been possible."

The Hertfordshire batteries seem to have made no effort to record the names of those who lost their lives while serving, still less place any form of memorial in Hertfordshire. A memorial was placed in the artillery drill hall in Peterborough, but it is selective, in that it records only the names of the four other ranks of B/270 who were killed in action or died of wounds. Only after the Hertfordshire Yeomanry and Artillery Historical Trust published a detailed *Roll of Honour* in 1972 was the extent of 4th East Anglian Brigade's casualties apparent. A total of 55 officers and men from the 1st, 2nd and 3rd Line units are officially recognised as having lost their lives during the First World War. The campaign in Egypt and Palestine accounts for two officers and 37 other ranks but of these, only six other ranks were killed in action or died of wounds. These losses do not bear comparison with those of their infantry colleagues; 1st/1st Battalion The Hertfordshire Regiment lost over nine hundred officers and men in four years in France and Flanders and 1st/5th [97]

Plate 69 *The grave of Bombardier A. Pearce of A/270 in Cairo War Memorial Cemetery. Bombardier Pearce, of St. Albans, was among sixteen officers and men of 270 Brigade who died during the two months following the end of the war with Turkey of malaria or pneumonia contracted on active service.* (Regimental Collection)

Battalion The Bedfordshire Regiment, who experienced all the same battles as 270 Brigade and were at the same risk of the diseases of the Eastern Mediterranean lost two hundred all ranks in Egypt and Palestine. (The comparison between artillery brigade and infantry battalion is valid but should not be made directly. The war establishment of a field artillery brigade was 580 all ranks, as against nearly one thousand all ranks for an infantry battalion.) There is no reliable record of casualties amongst personnel who enlisted for service with 4th East Anglian Brigade but lost their lives after posting to other units.

A study of *Hertfordshire Yeomanry and Artillery Honours and Awards* shows that awards went exclusively to the fighting echelons of 270 Brigade. The system may therefore have been less than generous to the all important support echelons and also appears not to have fully recognised the part played in the breakthrough to final victory in September 1918. Services in [98] 2nd/4th East Anglian (348 Brigade) were virtually unrecognised but a very interesting

Plate 70 *Fitter Staff-Sergeant H.A. Jones, of Watford, who enlisted in 2nd Herts Battery in June 1908 and served with 4th East Anglian Brigade, R.F.A. and its successor units throughout the campaign in Egypt and Palestine. He was among the relatively few senior non-commissioned officers of the brigade who rejoined after the First World War and he continued to serve with 86th Field Brigade, R.A. until 1935.* (Regimental Collection)

award of the Meritorious Service Medal 'for Gallantry in the performance of Military Duty' (approximately equivalent to today's Queen's Gallantry Medal) was made to Corporal J. Ginn, then serving with 4th Reserve Brigade (which had absorbed 3rd/4th East Anglian Brigade), though it is not known whether he was a member of the permanent cadre or 'awaiting posting', or in what circumstances he gained his award. Extra-regimentally employed officers received an interesting variety of awards, mainly for services with other artillery units or at H.Q.s R.A., rather than in more general staff appointments.

The future of the Hertfordshire batteries in the post-war Territorial Force (soon to become the Territorial Army) was inextricably interwoven with the future of the Hertfordshire Yeomanry, the 1st Line regiment of which had shared the rigours of the Egypt–Palestine campaign with 270 Brigade. The Hertfordshire Yeomanry was not high enough in the precedence of Yeomanry regiments to retain its traditional mounted role (see Chapter 1) and was therefore due for 'change of arm'. At the same time, while there was little doubt that the two Hertfordshire batteries would remain field artillery, they would have to join another county – probably Suffolk – in order to form part of one of the new 4-battery field artillery brigades of 54th Divisional Artillery. The options available to the Hertfordshire Yeomanry, favourite among which, in War Office eyes, was amalgamation with the Bedfordshire Yeomanry to form an Army (i.e., non-divisional) field brigade, did not reach Hertfordshire Territorial Association until very late in January 1920. They were not discussed amongst the officers of the regiment until they assembled for a conference in London on 19th March 1920 "on the subject of the future of the Herts Yeomanry", at which the agenda items were:

"1. The possibility of re-forming the Herts Yeomanry as suggested by the Secretary of State for War.

2. Taking into consideration the fact that under the conditions published in the Daily Press the regiment, if re-formed, will be liable in two years' time, if not sooner, to be changed into

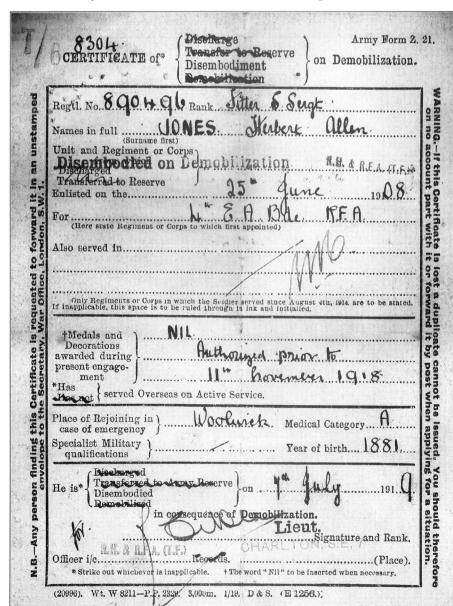

Plate 71 *Certificate of Disembodiment issued to Fitter Staff-Sergeant H.A. Jones on return to England in July 1919. He originally held the regimental number 99, reflecting his early enlistment into the Hertfordshire Batteries. This was changed to 890496 under the renumbering scheme for Territorial units of the Royal Field Artillery which took effect in February 1917. Although the certificate states that no medals had been authorised prior to 11th November 1918, he had in fact qualified for the 1914–15 Star.*
(Regimental Collection)

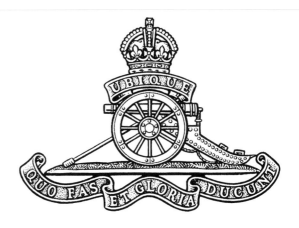

Plate 72   *The cap badge of the Royal Field Artillery after the substitution of the honour scroll 'Ubique' for the sprig of laurel (see Plate 5). In recognition of the part they played in the first three years of the war, Territorial units were authorised by Army Order 298 of 1917 to wear the honours accorded to their Regular counterparts.*   (Regimental Collection)

another Branch of the Service, whether it would not be better to come into line at once with the wishes of the General Staff and form with the two Hertfordshire Batteries of the late 4th East Anglian Brigade, R.F.A. one complete brigade of the Royal Field Artillery to bear the name of the county; the title of 'Yeomanry' to be borne by at least two batteries of the brigade."

At the meeting of Hertfordshire Territorial Association held on 12th April 1920, it was reported that the conference had unanimously agreed that it would be better to proceed at once with the raising of a complete field artillery brigade to be formed from the Hertfordshire Yeomanry and 1st and 2nd Hertfordshire Batteries, R.F.A. Application was accordingly made to the War Office the following day, stressing that the name of the county should be included in the unit's designation and that the traditions of the Yeomanry should be carried on by the use of the title 'Yeomanry' in some form or other. This request was accepted and at the next Association meeting it was reported that sanction had been given for the brigade to be raised, initially under the designation 3rd East Anglian Brigade, R.F.A. Two of the batteries would carry the title 'Hertfordshire Yeomanry'.

Meanwhile, recruiting for the post-war Territorial Force had begun in February 1920. Major Geoffrey Lawrence, D.S.O., the distinguished former commander of 1st/1st Hertfordshire Battery (A/270), was selected for command of the new brigade with the rank of lieutenant-colonel and his appointment, backdated to 16th February, was announced in the *London Gazette* of 1st April 1920. Four officers from the Hertfordshire Yeomanry joined 3rd East Anglian Brigade, two of them in command of the batteries that were expected to have Hertfordshire Yeomanry titles. Regrettably, there was little interest in their successor unit amongst former officers of 1st and 2nd Hertfordshire Batteries; only three transferred and the balance of key officer appointments was made up through Colonel Lawrence's careful selection of experienced Field Gunners from amongst those who applied. It is unfortunately not possible to say what proportion of the new brigade was formed from non-commissioned officers and men whose war service had been with either of the predecessor units but it may have been small. Administrative action was taken to release those officers of 4th East Anglian Brigade who did not volunteer for the post-war Territorial Force but had not yet resigned or retired. The names of three pre-war officers and 39 who were commissioned into the brigade during the war were listed in the *London Gazette* of 26th October 1921 as having relinquished their commissions with effect from 30th September.

The title of the new field artillery brigade was finally confirmed as 86th (East Anglian) (Hertfordshire Yeomanry) Brigade, Royal Field Artillery by Army Order 481 issued in December 1922. With the 'Yeomanry' designation now carried in the unit title, there was no attempt to repeat it at sub-unit (i.e., battery) level. The proposal that 86th Brigade should wear standard Royal Field Artillery uniform with the hart badge of the Hertfordshire Yeomanry on the shoulder strap was approved and, in common with all units of the Royal Field Artillery which traced their ancestry to the Yeomanry, non-commissioned officers and men of 86th Brigade wore the shoulder title Y. – R.F.A., rather than T. – R.F.A.

The history of 86th (East Anglian) (Hertfordshire Yeomanry) Brigade, Royal Field Artillery and the units, all carrying the 'Yeomanry' title, which sprang from it must be told in further volumes. It is however, appropriate to record here that 1st Northamptonshire Battery was re-formed as 336 Battery, R.F.A. and joined three Norfolk batteries in 84th Brigade, R.F.A., the successor unit to 1st East Anglian Brigade. When the three Norfolk batteries converted from the field to the anti-aircraft role in 1938, a happy chance placed 336 Battery alongside a Hertfordshire battery once more, and Gunners from the two counties went to war together again in 1939.

Appendix 1

Principal Acts of Parliament relating to the origin, raising and maintenance of Territorial units of the Royal Artillery, 1908–1920 and to the Volunteer Force, 1916–1920

1804 44 Geo.III c.54	*Volunteer Consolidation Act* Consolidates and amends earlier legislation. Authorises Yeomanry and Volunteer Corps already in existence to continue and provides for new corps to be formed. Yeomanry and Volunteers liable for call-out in case of "actual invasion or appearance of an enemy in force upon the coast" and to suppress riot or rebellion associated with invasion. Specifies four days' training every four months for mounted troops to be classified as 'efficient'. Enabling legislation for the Volunteer Force raised in 1859–60 until replaced by the Volunteer Act, 1863.
1863 26 & 27 Vict. c.65	*Volunteer Act* Authorises the Crown to accept offers of service of Volunteer Corps (other than the Yeomanry Cavalry, which continue to be raised under authority of 44 Geo. III c.54) and authorises corps accepted under earlier legislation to continue. Volunteers liable for call-out for "actual military service" in case of "actual or apprehended invasion" of any part of the United Kingdom but not specifically in the event of riot or civil commotion. Empowers the Secretary of State to make regulations covering the Volunteer Force. Requirements for certification as 'efficient' to be issued by Order in Council. Enabling legislation for the Volunteer Force from 1863 until Volunteer units were transferred to the Territorial Force in 1908. Remained in force and used as enabling legislation for the raising of a new Volunteer Force for Home Defence in 1916.
1907 7 Edw. VII c.9	*Territorial and Reserve Forces Act* Authorises the Crown to raise and maintain the Territorial Force consisting of such numbers of men as may be fixed by Parliament. Sets out the underlying provisions for administration by County Associations, organisation and training (maximum 18 days annually for mounted units) and provides for regulations to be issued by the Secretary of State. The Territorial Force to be embodied only after the call-out of the Army Reserve, and only for service in the United Kingdom, except in the case of those units or individuals who have volunteered to serve abroad. Units of the Imperial Yeomanry and the Volunteer Force to be transferred to the Territorial Force by Order in Council once the administrative machinery has been established in their counties.[1] Enables the

enlistment of men who have not served in the Regular Forces into the Army Reserve as 'Special Reservists'. Provides for the transfer by Order in Council of units of the Militia to the Special Reserve.

The Volunteer Act, 1863 remains available for the raising of volunteer forces in addition to the Territorial Force.

1916   *Volunteer Act*
6 & 7 Geo.V c.62   Authorises the acceptance of offers by individual members of Volunteer Corps to enter into agreements involving duties additional to those required under the Volunteer Act, 1863 for the duration of the present war.

NOTE
 1. Order in Council dated 19th March 1908 published as A.O. 70/1908 and in the *London Gazette* of 20th March 1908.

Appendix 2

War Establishments

The 4-Gun 15-pdr. Battery

The substantive War Establishment for a Territorial field battery included in *War Establishments, Part II, Territorial Force*, issued with Army Order 266 of 1911 (see Table 1), was identical to the Provisional War Establishment issued with Army Order 17 of 1909, and it was on this establishment that the Hertfordshire and Northamptonshire batteries mobilised in August 1914. The establishment for a battery was revised in June 1915 (*War Establishments, Part VIII, Territorial Divisions – 1st Line*, issued with Army Order 270 of 1915), when the number of subaltern officers was reduced from three to two. At the same time, one 'cart, cooks' was added to the establishment of 1st Line vehicles and the water cart was moved from 2nd Line transport ('Train') to 1st Line. The June 1915 establishment was revised again in November 1915 (Army Order 440 of 1915), still on the basis of four 15-pdr. B.L.C. guns. By this time, however, batteries of 1st/4th East Anglian Brigade had been re-equipped with four 18-pdr. guns each and would have adopted an 18-pdr. establishment similar to that shown in Table 2.

Reserve, later 2nd Line, Territorial batteries were first raised on the 1911 War Establishment. Separate establishments for 2nd Line units were not promulgated until September 1915 (as *War Establishments, Part IX, Territorial Divisions – 2nd Line*, issued with Army Order 398 of 1915). As far as field artillery batteries were concerned, the 2nd Line establishments did not differ significantly from those of the 1st Line.

The 4-Gun 18-pdr. Battery

As indicated above, the batteries of 1st/4th East Anglian Brigade would have adopted a 4-gun 18-pdr. establishment before moving to France in November 1915. It may be assumed that the Part VIII establishment issued in November 1915 was used; a Part VIII establishment specific to the 18-pdr. was not issued until February 1916 (Army Order 76 of 1916). Certainly, instructions were issued in January 1916 for Territorial divisions taking part in operations in Egypt – where 1st/4th East Anglian Brigade arrived in February – to conform to *War Establishments, Part VIII*, subject to certain amendments. These included an overall statement implying that mules might be issued in lieu of draught horses, though they were never, in practice, issued for gun draught, and substitute establishments for field artillery brigades, both gun and howitzer, and for divisional ammunition columns. In fact, as can be seen by comparing Tables 1 and 2, there was no significant difference between the establishment for a 4-gun 18-pdr. battery and that for the old 15-pdr. battery. The establishment shown in Table 2 held good until the reorganisation of field artillery brigades in Egypt, which took place in December 1916 (see page 49).

The batteries of 2nd/4th East Anglian Brigade (from May 1916, 348 Brigade), which had four 18-pdrs. each from mid-January 1916 until reorganisation began in November 1916, were on a similar establishment to that shown in Table 2.

The 6-Gun 18-pdr. Battery

Some two years of war experience resulted in the issue in July 1916 of Section 313 of *War Establishments, Part VII, General*, covering field artillery brigades. Batteries of 18-pdr. guns could have either six or four guns, while 4.5-in. howitzer batteries would have four guns. These batteries could be grouped under a brigade headquarters in five different combinations. There was no longer provision for a brigade ammunition column, the duties of which were [103] assumed by an expanded divisional ammunition column, to which personnel, horses and vehicles of the old brigade columns were transferred.

It is likely that the reorganisation of 273 Brigade (formerly 1st/4th East Anglian Brigade) into 270 Brigade, on the establishment for a brigade consisting of two 6-gun 18-pdr. batteries and one 4-gun 4.5-in. howitzer battery, which took place in December 1916 (see page 49), was as detailed in *War Establishments, Part VII, General*. A similar establishment specific to the Egypt–Palestine theatre does not appear to have been issued until August 1917, when it was promulgated as Section 699/42 of *War Establishments, Part XI, Egypt*. The difference between the equivalent tables in *Part VII* and *Part XI* is in any case negligible, consisting, as it does, of only one trumpeter in the establishment of a field battery of very nearly two hundred all ranks. The *Part XI* establishment shown in Table 3 remained in force until after the armistice with Turkey. Accordingly, it and its *Part VII* predecessor were the only establishments under which the Hertfordshire batteries were in active operations against the enemy, though in the early months of 1917 they had been considerably altered by the move to camel transport and the reduction to four guns to allow double teams (see page 51).

The reorganisation of 348 Brigade to an establishment of three 6-gun 18-pdr. batteries and one 4-gun 4.5-in. howitzer battery in November–December 1916 (see page 91) appears also to have been in accordance with *War Establishments, Part VII, General* and so would have followed Table 3. The establishment of batteries serving at home was reduced in September 1917, though it is not clear whether the reduction was due to shortage of men or horses, or both, or some other reason. Section 697 of *Part VII*, promulgated in September 1917 and covering 'Field Artillery Brigades (Home)', details only nine 4-horse ammunition wagons per battery, with eighteen drivers and 36 horses – a considerable saving on the previous twelve 6-horse wagons with 36 drivers and 72 horses. These reductions were continued in establishments issued in March 1918 as *War Establishments, Part XIV, Home Service* (Section 1099/29) and evidently held good for the rest of the war.

Table 1

A Field Artillery Battery, Territorial Force (Four 15-pdr. B.L.C. guns), 1911

Personnel and Horses

	Officers	Warrant Officers, Staff-Sgts. and Sergeants	Artificers	Rank and File[a]	Total	Riding Horses	Draught Horses
Major	1	..	..	..	1	2	..
Captain	1	..	..	..	1	2	..
Subalterns	3	..	..	..	3	6	..
Battery Sergeant-Major	..	1	..	..	1	1	..
Battery Quarter-master-Sergeant	..	1	..	..	1	1	..
Sergeants	..	5	..	..	5	5	..
Farrier-Sergeant	..	..	1	..	1	1	..
Shoeing-Smiths	..	..	3[b]	..	3	1	..
Saddlers	..	..	2	..	2	..	..
Fitters/Wheelers	..	..	2	..	2	..	..
Trumpeters	..	..	..	2	2	2	..
Corporals	..	..	..	5	5	}	..
Bombardiers	..	..	..	9	9 }[c]	19[d]	..
Gunners	..	..	..	52	52 }	..	..
Drivers, for vehicles	..	..	..	36	36	..	72
Drivers, for spare horses	..	..	..	7	7	6	8
Drivers, spare	..	..	..	4	4	..	..
Batmen[e]	..	..	..	10	10	..	..
Total	5	7	8	125	145	46	80

Guns and 1st Line Vehicles[g]

	Guns/Vehicles	Drivers	Draught Horses	Riding Horses
Carriages, gun, with limbers	4	12	24	..
Wagons, ammunition, with limbers	8	24	48	..
Drivers, for spare horses	..	7	8	6
Total	12	47	80	6

NOTES

a. Includes six acting bombardiers
b. Includes one corporal
c. Includes two look-out men
d. Composed as follows:
   Ground scouts 2
   Observing party, including range-takers 6[f]
   Mounted orderly 1
   Battery commander's signallers 3[f]
   Patrol 3[f]
   Coverers 4
   19

e. All batmen are fully equipped and trained soldiers and are available for duty in the ranks.
f. Includes horse-holders
g. 2nd Line transport consisting of one water cart and two wagons "for baggage, stores and supplies" was to be requisitioned on mobilisation and would be provided with drivers by the Divisional Train, Army Service Corps.

[Source: *War Establishments, Part II – Territorial Force, 1911*]

Table 2

A Field Artillery Battery, Territorial Force (1st Line)(Four 18-pdr.Q.F. guns), 1916

Personnel and Horses

	Officers	Warrant Officers, Staff-Sgts. and Sergeants	Artificers	Rank and File[a]	Total	Riding Horses	Draught Horses
Major	1	..	..	..	1	2	..
Captain	1	..	..	..	1	2	..
Subalterns	2	..	..	..	2	4	..
Battery Sergeant-Major	..	1	..	..	1	1	..
Battery Quarter-master-Sergeant	..	1	..	..	1	1	..
Sergeants	..	5	..	..	5	5	..
Farrier-Sergeant	..	..	1	..	1	1	..
Shoeing-Smiths	..	..	3[b]	..	3	1	..
Saddlers	..	..	2	..	2	..	..
Fitters/Wheelers	..	..	2	..	2	..	..
Trumpeters	..	..	..	2	2	2	..
Corporals	..	..	..	5	5	..	..
Bombardiers	..	..	..	9	9 } [c]	21[d]	..
Gunners	..	..	..	51	51	..	..
Drivers, for vehicles	..	..	..	38	38	..	75
Drivers, for spare horses	..	..	..	6	6	4	8
Drivers, spare	..	..	..	2	2	..	..
Batmen[e]	..	..	..	8	8	..	..
Total	**4**	**7**	**8**	**121**	**140**	**44**	**83**

Guns and 1st Line Vehicles[g]

	Guns/Vehicles	Drivers	Draught Horses	Riding Horses
Carriages, gun, with limbers	4	12	24	..
Wagons, ammunition, with limbers	8	24	48	..
Carts, cooks	1	1	1	..
Carts, water	1	1	2	..
Drivers, for spare horses	..	7	8	6
Drivers, spare	..	5	..	..
Bicycles[h]	1	..	..	..
Total	**15**	**50**	**83**	**6**

NOTES

a. Includes six acting bombardiers
b. Includes one corporal
c. Includes two look-out men and 21 N.C.Os. and men trained as telephonists; nine of the latter to be further trained in the use of the buzzer and eight in signalling
d. Composed as follows:

Orderlies	3[f]
Signallers	7[f]
Look-out men	2
Range-takers	2[f]
Patrol	3[f]
Coverers	4
	21

e. All batmen are fully equipped and trained soldiers and are available for duty in the ranks.
f. Includes horse-holders
g. 2nd Line or 'Train' transport consisting of three 2-horse General Service wagons – two for "baggage stores and supplies" and one for "extra forage" – with drivers, was attached from the Divisional Train, Army Service Corps.
h. Riders to be detailed as necessary

[Source: *War Establishments, Part VIII – Territorial Divisions – 1st Line, February 1916*]

Table 3

A Field Artillery Battery (Six 18-pdr. Q.F. guns), Egypt, 1917[a]

Personnel and Horses

	Officers	Warrant Officers, Staff-Sgts. and Sergeants	Artificers	Rank and File[b]	Total	Riding Horses	Draught Horses
Major	1	..	..	..	1	2	..
Captain	1	..	..	..	1	2	..
Subalterns	3	..	..	..	3	6	..
Battery Sergeant-Major	..	1	..	..	1	1	..
Battery Quarter-master-Sergeant	..	1	..	..	1	1	..
Sergeants	..	7	..	..	7	7	..
Farrier-Sergeant	..	..	1	..	1	1	..
Shoeing-Smiths	..	..	4[c]	..	4	1	..
Saddlers	..	..	2	..	2	..	..
Fitters/Wheelers	..	..	2	..	2	..	..
Trumpeter	..	..	..	1	1	1	..
Corporals	..	..	..	7	7	..	..
Bombardiers	..	..	..	11	11 [d]	21[e]	..
Gunners	..	..	..	75	75	..	
Drivers, for vehicles	..	..	..	56	56	..	111
Drivers, for spare horses				9	9	6	12
Drivers, spare				6	6	..	..
Batmen				10	10	..	..
Total[g]	5	9	9	175	198	49	123

Guns and 1st Line Vehicles[h]

	Guns/Vehicles	Drivers	Draught Horses	Riding Horses
Carriages, gun, with limbers	6	18	36	..
Wagons, ammunition, with limbers	12	36	72	..
Carts, cooks	1	1	1	..
Carts, water	1	1	2	..
Drivers, for spare horses	9	12	6	6
Drivers, spare	..	6	..	..
Bicycles[j]	1	..	..	..
Total	21	71	123	6

NOTES

a. This establishment remained in force until November 1918.

b. Includes nine acting bombardiers

c. Includes one corporal

d. Includes two look-out men and 21 N.C.Os. and men trained as signallers

e. Allotted as follows:

Ground scouts	2
Orderly	1
Signallers	6[f]
Range-takers	3[f]
Patrol	3[f]
Coverers	6
	21

f. Includes horse-holders

g. Two men per battery are trained in sanitary duties

h. 2nd Line or 'Train' transport consisting of two 4-horse General Service wagons for "baggage stores and supplies", with drivers, was attached from the Divisional Train, Army Service Corps. Fifty per cent of the Train drivers were locally enlisted native personnel.

j. Riders to be detailed as necessary

[Source: *War Establishments, Part XI – Egypt – No. 699/42, August 1917*]

ROYAL FIELD ARTILLERY.

Northamptonshire Battery, 4th East Anglian Brigade; the undermentioned officers, from the 1st Volunteer Battalion, The Northamptonshire Regiment, are appointed to the battery, with rank and precedence as in the Volunteer Force. Dated 1st April, 1908 :—

Major and Honorary Lieutenant-Colonel (Captain, Reserve of Officers) John Thomas Woolrych Perowne.

Captain Harry Hamilton Staton.

Captain Sidney George Cook. (To be supernumerary).

Lieutenant (Honorary Lieutenant in the Army) Thomas Henry Walker.

Lieutenant Francis Edmond Crawshay Stanley.

Lieutenant Robert Alexander Walker.

1st Hertfordshire Battery, 4th East Anglian Brigade; Captain Osmond Robert McMullen, from the 1st (Hertfordshire) Volunteer Battalion, The Bedfordshire Regiment, to be Major. Dated 19th May, 1908.

Julian Urban Smith to be Second Lieutenant. Dated 19th May, 1908.

2nd Hertfordshire Battery, 4th East Anglian Brigade; Edward Alec Horsman Bailey to be Second Lieutenant. Dated 2nd July, 1908.

George Robertson Holland to be Second Lieutenant. Dated 3rd July, 1908.

Plate 73 *The announcements of the first commissions in 4th East Anglian Brigade as they appeared in the 'London Gazette'. The transfer of six officers from 1st Volunteer Battalion The Northamptonshire Regiment to 1st Northamptonshire Battery were gazetted on 8th September 1908 but with an effective date of 1st April 1908. Appointments to the Hertfordshire batteries were not gazetted until 10th November 1908, again with earlier effective dates. Only one officer, Captain O.R. McMullen, transferred from the Volunteer Force to the Hertfordshire batteries. Officers' first appointments and all subsequent promotions, secondments, appointments to the staff, etc. were (and indeed, still are) published in the 'London Gazette', which with the 'Army List', is an invaluable reference source. No such publicly available information exists for other ranks.*

Appendix 3

Extracts from the Monthly Army List

1. September 1909

4th East Anglian Brigade.
[55]
28, St. Andrew's Street,
Hertford.
Hon. Colonel.
✗Salisbury, Rt. Hon.,
J. E. H., Marq. of,
G.C.V.O., C.B., TD,
Lt.-Col. 4 Bn. Bedf.
R., Col., A.D.C.
(*H*)   17Feb.09

Lt.-Colonel.
✗Foot, R. M. (*Maj.
Res. of Off.*) 17Feb.09

Orderly Officer.

Adjutant.
Dunbar, J. C.,
Capt. R. Art. 1Sept.08

1st *Hertfordshire Battery.*
26, St. Andrew's Street,
Hertford.
Major.
McMullen, O. R.
                19May08
Captain.
Bowden, G.R.H.9June09

Lieutenants. (2)

2nd Lieutenant. (1)
Smith, J. U.   19May08

2nd *Hertfordshire Battery.*
Watford.
Major.

Captain.
Holland, G. R. 23Apr.09

Lieutenants. (2)

2nd Lieutenant. (1).
Bailey, E. A. H. 2July08
Strode, G. W.   11Dec.08

Northamptonshire *Battery.*
Drill Hall, Queen's Road.
Peterborough.
Major.
p.s. Perowne, J.T.W.,
vd., *hon. l.c.*
(*Capt. Res. of
Off.*) (Q) ③ (*H*)
                3Dec.04
Captain.
p.s. Cook, S.G.   7Jan.05
Lieutenants. (2)
p.✗Walker, T. H.
(*Hon. Lt. in
Army* 18 July
02)   23Sept.01
p.s. Stanley, F.E.C.
(*H*)   13Aug.04
2nd Lieutenant. (1)
Edmonds, G. M. 14Apr.09

The brigade has been in existence for over a year and the three batteries are well established. Lieutenant-Colonel R.M. Foot has been appointed as the first commanding officer but 2nd Herts Battery still lack a battery commander in the rank of major. The post of Honorary Colonel, which had become established in the later years of the Volunteer Force, has been continued in the Territorial Force and Colonel The Marquess of Salisbury has been appointed to the vacancy in the new unit. As a result of the continuing difficulties in forming the brigade ammunition column, this sub-unit is not yet shown.

The crossed-swords symbol indicates that officers have previous active service experience; all those marked fought in South Africa.

The unit's precedence, 55th, shown in brackets below the title, is lowest amongst the divisional artillery brigades and reflects the absence of artillery units in Hertfordshire and Northamptonshire before 1908.

2. October 1912

4th East Anglian Brigade.

[55]

28, St. Andrew's Street, Hertford.

Hon. Colonel.
✕Salisbury, Rt. Hon., J. E. H., Marq. of, G.C.V.O., C.B., TD, Lt.-Col. 4 Bn. Bedf. R., Col., A.D.C. (H)   17 Feb. 09

Lt.-Colonel.
✕Foot, R. M. (*Maj. Res. of Off.*)   17 Feb. 09

Orderly Officer.

Adjutant.
✕Bourchier, R. W. H., Capt. R.A.   1 Sept. 11

Chaplain.
Chaplin, *Rev.* A., Chapl. 4'h Class (T.F.) (*attd.*) 1 July 12

1st *Hertfordshire Battery*.

Artillery Buildings, Harpenden Road, St. Albans.

Major.
Bowden, G. R. H.   1 July 12

Captain.
Smith, J. U.   1 July 12

Lieutenants. (2)
Bates, K. L.   15 June 12

2nd Lieutenant. (1)
Lydekker, C. J.   1 Oct. 10

2nd *Hertfordshire Battery*.

Clarendon Hall, Watford

Major.
Holland, G. P.   1 June 12

Captain
Bailey, E. A. H.   1 June 12

Lieutenants. (2)
Agnew, A. G.   15 June 12

2nd Lieutenant. (1)
Foot, R. C.   23 Mar. 12

———

Cadet Unit affiliated.
2nd Hertfordshire (Watford Scouts) Cadet Company.

Northamptonshire Battery.

Drill Hall, Queen's Street, Peterborough.

Major.
Exeter, W. T. B., *Marq. of, late* Capt. 3 Bn. North'n R.   7 May 10

Captain.
p. Walker, T. H. (*Hon. Lt. in Army* 18 *July* 02)   1 May 11

Lieutenants. (2)
p.s. Stanley, F.E.C. (H)   13 Aug. 04
Philips, C. J. H.   15 June 12

2nd Lieutenant. (1)

4th East Anglian Ammunition Column.

28, St. Andrew's Street, Hertford.

Captain.

Lieutenants (2).
Newton, A. D. 15 June 12

2nd Lieutenants (2).

The brigade is now in its fifth year and its entry in the monthly Army List is similar in all respects to those of other divisional artillery brigades. The brigade ammunition column, recognised by the Army Council in May 1910, now has an entry, though it still lacks four officers. Full addresses are now given for all three batteries and the ammunition column, and the move of 1st Herts Battery from Hertford to St. Albans is confirmed.

The 2nd Hertfordshire (Watford Scouts) Cadet Company was raised in April 1911 and affiliated to 2nd Herts Battery, the only cadet company in Hertfordshire with an artillery affiliation. In November 1913, however, the affiliation was changed to 1st Battalion The Hertfordshire Regiment and it was to be over forty years before Hertfordshire cadets would once more be affiliated to the Royal Artillery.

3. November 1914

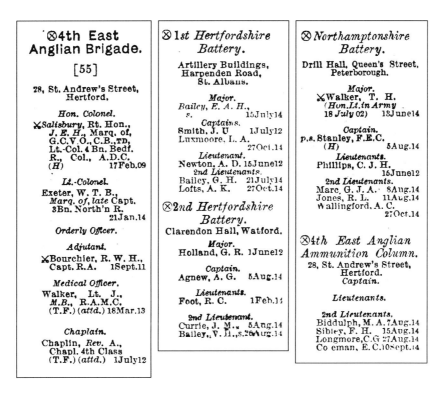

⊗4th East Anglian Brigade.

[55]

28, St. Andrew's Street, Hertford.

Hon. Colonel.
✗Salisbury, Rt. Hon., J. E. H., Marq. of, G.C.V.O., C.B.,TD, Lt.-Col. 4 Bn. Bedf. R., Col., A.D.C. (H) 17Feb.09

Lt.-Colonel.
Exeter, W. T. B., *Marq. of, late* Capt. 3Bn. North'n R. 21Jan.14

Orderly Officer.

Adjutant.
✗Bourchier, R. W. H., Capt. R.A. 1Sept.11

Medical Officer.
Walker, Lt. J., M.B., R.A.M.C. (T.F.) (*attd.*) 18Mar.13

Chaplain.
Chaplin, *Rev.* A., Chapl. 4th Class (T.F.) (*attd.*) 1July12

⊗ 1st *Hertfordshire Battery*.

Artillery Buildings, Harpenden Road, St. Albans.

Major.
Bailey, E. A. H., s. 15July14
Captains.
Smith, J. U 1July12
Luxmoore, L. A. 27Oct.14
Lieutenant.
Newton, A. D. 15June12
2nd Lieutenants.
Bailey, G. H. 21July14
Lofts, A. K. 27Oct.14

⊗2nd *Hertfordshire Battery*.
Clarendon Hall, Watford.

Major.
Holland, G. R. 1June12

Captain.
Agnew, A. G. 5Aug.14

Lieutenants.
Foot, R. C. 1Feb.14

2nd Lieutenant.
Currie, J. M. 5Aug.14
Bailey, V. H., s. 26Aug.14

⊗ *Northamptonshire Battery*.

Drill Hall, Queen's Street, Peterborough.

Major.
✗Walker, T. H. *(Hon.Lt.in Army* 18 *July* 02) 13June14

Captain.
p.s. Stanley, F.E.C. (H) 5Aug.14
Lieutenants.
Phillips, C. J. H. 16June12
2nd Lieutenants.
Marc, G. J. A. 8Aug.14
Jones, R. L. 11Aug.14
Wallingford, A. C. 27Oct.14

⊗4th East Anglian Ammunition Column.
28, St. Andrew's Street, Hertford.
Captain.

Lieutenants.

2nd Lieutenants.
Biddulph, M. A. 7Aug.14
Sibley, F. H. 15Aug.14
Longmore, C.G 27Aug.14
Coleman, E. C. 10Sept.14

The brigade has been embodied and mobilised and all three batteries and the ammunition column have been accepted for Imperial Service, as indicated by the symbol to the left of the unit and sub-unit titles. A number of officers have been commissioned since the outbreak of war. Major E.A.H. Bailey of 1st Herts Battery, now shown in italic type and with 's' beside his name, has been seconded to a staff appointment, while his brother, 2nd Lieutenant V.H. Bailey, is occupying a minor staff appointment without being seconded.

4. November 1916

4th East Anglian Brigade.
[55]
28, St. Andrew's Street,
Hertford.
Hon. Colonel.
XSalisbury, Rt. Hon.,
J. E. H., Marq. of,
G.C.V.O., C.B., TD,
Col., A.D.C. (H)
17Feb.09
Lt.-Colonel.
1Exeter, W. T. B.,
Marq. of, late Capt.,
3Bn North'n R.
21Jan.14
Orderly Officer.
1Sibley, F. H., 2nd Lt.
16Aug.14
Adjutant
Bailey, V. H., 2nd Lt.
(*Lt.)   12May16
Medical Officer.
1Walker, Capt. J.,
M.B., R.A.M.C.
(T.F.) (attd.) 1Apr.15
18Mar.18
Chaplain.
1Chaplin, Rev. A.,
Chapl. 4th Class
(T.F.) (attd.) 1July12

4th East Anglian
Brigade—*contd.*
"A" Battery
(1st Hertfordshire).
Artillery Buildings,
Harpenden Road,
St. Albans.
Majors.
Batley, E. A. H., s.
16July15
1Lawrence, G.   *2May15
Captain.
1Allhusen, O.   *21May15
*17Nov.16
Lieutenants.
1Harris, F.   *1Mar.15
2nd Lieutenants.
1Coleman, E. C. (*Lt.
21 Jan. 15) 10Sept.14
c. Lofts, A. K. (*Capt.
2 Oct. 15) 27Oct.14
1Lutyens, E. J. T.
20Nov.14
3Stubbs, T. W. (*Lt.
18 May 16 (Instnl.
Duties) 3Apr.15
Weber, R E. (*Capt.
whilst attd. 3 N. Mid.
Brig. R.F.A.
23 Feb. 16) 16Apr.15
1Phillips, A. A. H.
(*Lt. 18 Jan. 16)
27Apr.15
3Kay, H. G. A. 29Aug.15
2Bagshawe,E.N.14Oct.15
2Perkins, E. C. 3Nov.15

"B" Battery
(2nd Hertfordshire).
Clarendon Hall, Watford.
Major.
3Holland,G.R.   1June15
Captain.
2Smith, J. U.   1July15
Lieutenants.
3Foot, R. C. (*Capt.
27 June 15) 1Feb.16
2nd Lieutenants.
1Currie, J. M. (*Capt.
29 Sept. 15) 5Aug.14
1Earford, W. G. 9Dec.14
1Cowley, J. N. 16Feb.15
2Watson, J. A. S. (*Lt.
4 June 16) 25July15
2Clayton, T. W. (*Lt.
1 Oct. 16) 13Aug.16
1Gorman, J. K. (*Lt.
22 Sept. 15) 22Sept.15
*5Apr.15
3Lake, A. H.   12Oct.15
2Williams, E. H.17Oct.15
2Rider, W. H.   6Nov.15

"C" Battery
(Northamptonshire).
Drill Hall, Queen's Street
Peterborough.
Major.
1XWalker, T. K.
(Hon.Lt.in Army
15 July 02) 13June14
Captain.
1p.s.Stanley, F. E. C.
(*Maj. 6 Aug. 16)
(H) 4Aug.16
Lieutenants.
c. Phillips, C. J. H.
15June15
1Newton, A. D. (*Capt.
27 July 16) 15June12

2nd Lieutenants.
1Longmore, C. G.
27Aug.14
2Wallingford, A. C.
(*Capt. 8 July 15)
27Oct.14
3Phelips, G. E. F.
(*Capt.4Feb.16) 6Jan.15
2XPonsonby, H. P.5May15
2Lawrance,N.M. 9June15
3Bagshawe, C. R. V.
20Aug.15
2Tanner, G.   14Oct.15
1Nelson, E.G.S. 29Oct.15

**4th East Anglian
Ammunition Column.**
28, St. Andrew's Street,
Hertford.
Captain.
Lieutenant.
2nd Lieutenants.
Biddulph, M. A.
7Aug.14
1Mare, G. J. A. 8Aug.14
3Jones, R. L. (*Capt.
6 June 15) 11Aug.14
1Bailey, V. H. (*Lt.
7Dec.14)Adjt. 26Aug.14
1Croft, P. R. (*Capt.
4 Oct. 15) 21Sept.14
Terrell A. & B. K.
(*Lt.29June15)20Nov.14
1Smith, M.   16Feb.15
2Balme, C. (*Lt.
4 June 16 16May15
1Taylor, J. W. A.23July15
1Wheeler, F. O. 3Sept.15
2Phillips, P. R. (*Lt.
1 Oct. 16) 18Sept.15
1Leonard, G. J. F.
19Oct.15
3Russell, G. G. 3Dec.15
3Walker, N.   16Dec.15
Plant, C. H.   23Dec.15
3Pryor, T. S.   31Dec.15

Unposted.
Major.
Corlette, H. C. (H)
(Q) sp. emp. *14Nov.15
11June14
Lieutenant.
2Ritchie, W., 2nd Lt.
R.F.A.   *16Dec.15
2nd Lieutenants.
XDrinkwater, G. C.
(*Lt. 6 May 15) s
27Jan.15
2Mollison, R.W.20Dec.15
1Mathew, D. H. 28Dec.15
2Cowie, W. E. C.16Apr.16
3Beeston, C. G. 22July16
3Harris, D. R. 27Aug.16
3Mercer, F.   2Sept.16
3Davy, F. E.   12Nov.16

Most officers have been commissioned since the outbreak of war. They are now annotated '1', '2', '3' or 'C' to show whether they are serving with the 1st, 2nd or 3rd Line unit or at the brigade depot. Those seconded to staff appointments or for service with other units are shown in italic type.

The original title of the brigade has been retained, despite the change in title of the 1st and 2nd Line units in May 1916 to 273 Brigade and 348 Brigade, respectively. The batteries have been given the lettered designations introduced at the same time.

Individual brigades of the Royal Field Artillery, T.F. ceased to be shown in the *Monthly Army List* after March 1917.

Bibliography and Guide to Sources

PRINTED BOOKS

BAKER, H. *The Territorial Force – A Manual of its Law, Organisation and Administration*, London, John Murray, 1909.

BARNETT, C. *Britain and Her Army 1509–1970 – A Military, Political and Social Survey*, London, Alan Lane (The Penguin Press), 1970.

BECKE, A.F. *Order of Battle of Divisions 1914–1918* (6 Vols.), London, H.M.S.O., 1934–1945.

BECKETT, I.F.W. *The Amateur Military Tradition 1558–1945*, Manchester, Manchester University Press, 1992.

BECKETT, I.F.W. and SIMPSON, K. (Eds.) *A Nation in Arms – A social study of the British Army in the First World War*, Manchester, Manchester University Press, 1985.

BIDWELL, R.G.S. *Gunners at War – A Tactical Study of the Royal Artillery in the Twentieth Century*, London, Arms and Armour Press, 1970.

BLACKWELL, E. and AXE, E.C. *Romford to Beirut . . . An Outline of the War Record of B Battery, 271 Brigade, R.F.A. . . .*, Clacton-on-Sea, Essex, R.W. Humphris, 1926.

BULLOCK, D.L. *Allenby's War – The Palestine–Arabian Campaigns 1916–1918*, London, Blandford Press, 1988.

CAMPBELL, D.A. *The Dress of the Royal Artillery*, London, Arms and Armour Press, 1971.

CHAPPELL, M. *British Cavalry Equipments 1800–1941*, London, Osprey Publishing Ltd., 1983.

COUSINS, G. *The Defenders – A History of the British Volunteer*, London, Frederick Muller Ltd., 1968.

CUNNINGHAM, H. *The Volunteer Force – A Social and Political History 1859–1908*, London, Croom Helm Ltd., 1975.

DENNIS, P. *The Territorial Army 1906–1940*, Woodbridge, Suffolk, Boydell Press (for the Royal Historical Society), 1987.

DUNLOP, J.K. *The Development of the British Army 1899–1914*, London, Methuen and Co., 1938.

FARNDALE, M. *History of the Royal Regiment of Artillery – The Forgotton Fronts and the Home Base, 1914–18*, London, Royal Artillery Institution, 1988.

FREDERICK, J.B.M. *The Lineage Book of British Land Forces 1660–1978* (2 Vols.), Wakefield, Yorkshire, Microform Academic Publishers, 1986.

GRIFFITH, A.L.P. *A Brief Record of the Hertfordshire Yeomanry and the Hertfordshire Artillery*, Hertford, G. Creasey and Sons, 1927.

HOGG, I.V. *A History of Artillery*, London, Hamlyn Publishing Group Ltd., 1974

LOWE, P.A. *The Development of Artillery Tactics since 1900*, Tactics Wing, Royal School of Artillery, 1976.

LUTYENS, E.J.T. *With the Herts Gunners (1914–1918)*, [published privately, 1930].

MACMUNN, Sir G. and FALLS, C. *History of the Great War: Military Operations – Egypt and Palestine 1914–1918* (3 Vols. + Maps, etc.), London, H.M.S.O., 1928–1930.

MAURICE-JONES, K.W. *The History of Coast Artillery in the British Army*, London, Royal Artillery Institution, 1959.

RICHARDS, W. *His Majesty's Territorial Army* (4 Vols.), London, Virtue and Co., n.d. [c.1910].

ROBSON, B. *Swords of the British Army – The Regulation Patterns 1788–1914*, London, Arms and Armour Press, 1975.

SAINSBURY, J.D. *Hertfordshire's Soldiers from 1757*, Hitchin, Hertfordshire, Hertfordshire Local History Council, 1969.

SAINSBURY, J.D. *Roll of Honour of Officers and Men of Hertfordshire Yeomanry and Artillery Units who lost their lives on active service in South Africa and in the two World Wars*, Digswell, Hertfordshire, Hertfordshire Yeomanry and Artillery Historical Trust, 1972 (First Supplement, 1977; Second and Final Supplement, 1982).

SAINSBURY, J.D. *A Record of Honours and Awards to Officers and Men of Hertfordshire Yeomanry and Artillery Units*, Digswell, Hertfordshire, Hertfordshire Yeomanry and Artillery Historical Trust, 1977 (First Supplement, 1984; Second and Final Supplement in preparation).

SAINSBURY, J.D. *A Short Account of the Volunteer Artillery*, Journal of the Royal Artillery, Volume XCIII, No.1 – Spring 1966.

SELLWOOD, A.V. *The Saturday Night Soldiers – The Stirring Story of the Territorial Army*, London, White Lion Publishers Ltd., 1974 (2nd Edition).

SMITH, D.J. *Discovering Horse-Drawn Transport of the British Army*, Princes Risborough, Shire Publications Ltd., 1977.

STANLEY, F.E.C. and others *A Short History of the Northamptonshire Battery (B/270, R.F.A.)* Peterborough, Peterborough Press Ltd. [printers], 1926.

TYLDEN, G. *Horses and Saddlery – An account of the animals used by the British and Commonwealth Armies . . . with a description of their equipment*, London, J.A. Allen and Co., 1965.

WALLACE, E. *Kitchener's Army and the Territorial Forces*, London, George Newnes Ltd., n.d. [1915].

WEBSTER, F.A.M. *The History of the 5th Battalion The Bedfordshire and Hertfordshire Regiment (T.A.)*, London, F. Warne & Co. Ltd., 1930.

A Brief Record of the Advance of the Egyptian Expeditionary Force July 1917 to October 1918, London, H.M.S.O., 1919.

Officers Died in the Great War 1914–1919, London, H.M.S.O., 1919.

Soldiers died in the Great War 1914–1919. Part 2: Royal Horse and Royal Field Artillery – Section 6 (Territorial Force), London, H.M.S.O., 1921.

The Territorial Year Book – 1909, London, Hodder and Stoughton, 1909.

PARLIAMENTARY PAPERS, ETC.

Annual Return of the Territorial Force, 1908–1913.

Return of the Territorial Force at Home, August 1914–June 1917.

Return of the British Army at Home, July 1917–December 1918.

Reports of Proceedings at a Conference between the Secretary of State for War and Representatives of the Territorial Force Associations (3 pamphlets recording conferences which took place on 1st April 1919, 1st May 1919 and 30th January 1920).

Reorganisation of the Territorial Force (4-page leaflet outlining the arrangements. Printed for the War Office, February 1920).

Abstract of the Recommendations of Commissions, Committees and Conferences relating to Army Affairs (Vol.2: 1900–1920).

REGULATIONS, TRAINING PUBLICATIONS, ETC.

Regulations for the Territorial Force and for County Associations.
Handbook of the 15-pdr. B.L.C. Gun.
Handbook of the 18-pdr. Q.F. Gun.
Handbook of the 4.5-in. Q.F. Howitzer.
Establishments and *War Establishments.*

OTHER OFFICIAL PUBLICATIONS

The London Gazette.
Army Lists, especially the *Monthly Army List.*
Army Orders (formerly *General Orders*).
Army Council Instructions.

Notes: The *London Gazette* is registered as a newspaper and is held by a number of major public reference libraries.
Details of the various *Army Lists* and lists covering the Auxiliary Forces are given in WHITE, A.S. 'The Army List', *Journal of the Society for Army Historical Research*, Vol. XXV, No. 103 – Autumn 1947 and Vol. XLV – No. 181, Spring 1967.

Army Lists and the *Orders* and *Instructions* mentioned above were published by H.M.S.O. for the War Office and on publication were subject to varying degrees of security classification, and hence availability. In general these security classifications have now been removed and such copies as have reached public reference libraries are available without restriction. Readers requiring advice on these specialised sources are recommended to consult the National Army Museum (Department of Records).

NEWSPAPERS, ETC.

The Times.

Local newspapers published in Hertfordshire, especially the *Hertfordshire Mercury* (Hertford), *Hertfordshire Advertiser* (St. Albans), *Watford Observer* and *Hertfordshire Express* (Hitchin).

Watford Illustrated (available in Watford Library).

Hertfordshire Almanac (available in Hertford Library).

OTHER SOURCES

Public Record Office

War Diaries 1914–1919: 1st/4th East Anglian Brigade, R.F.A. (later 273 Brigade, then 270 Brigade) and 2nd/4th East Anglian Brigade, R.F.A. (later 348 Brigade) (W.O.95)

Hertfordshire County Record Office

Hertfordshire Territorial Force Association (later Territorial and Auxiliary Forces Association) – Minute Books and related Committee Papers 1908–1920.

Royal Artillery Institution, Woolwich

The extensive collections of the Royal Artillery Institution include duplicate war diaries for 1914–18, records of formation, disbandment, etc. of batteries and regiments, equipment handbooks and training publications and a wealth of other material relating to the Royal Regiment of Artillery, both Regular and Reserve.

The Regimental Collection

A substantial archive including private correspondence, diaries, programmes, etc. and photographs has been deposited at Hertfordshire County Record Office by the Hertfordshire Yeomanry and Artillery Historical Trust. It is catalogued under reference D/EYO.

About the Author

John Sainsbury was born in Hitchin in 1938 and educated first at local schools, including Hitchin Grammar School, and later at Eton. He was commissioned in the Royal Artillery during National Service, which he spent with a field regiment in Germany. On release from full-time service he joined the Bank of England, where he worked, initially in the Overseas and Economic Intelligence Departments, then in the Corporate Services Department, until retiring a few years early in 1989. He then spent nearly seven years as archivist in the Honours and Awards Branch of the Military Secretary's Department of the Ministry of Defence. As a Territorial Army officer he has served in local field artillery units and in a variety of staff appointments.

His interest in military history goes back to his school days but gained real purpose when, on joining the Hertfordshire Yeomanry – by then a field regiment of the Royal Artillery – he discovered how little had been published on the units of the Auxiliary Forces raised in the county. His first book – *Hertfordshire's Soldiers* – appeared in 1969 and several others have followed. *The Hertfordshire Batteries, Royal Field Artillery – An Illustrated History 1908–1920* joins similar works on Hertfordshire's Territorial Infantry and the Hertfordshire Yeomanry in a series which the author regards as a major step towards increasing public awareness of the continuing history and achievements of local units. He looks forward to producing further volumes on Hertfordshire's Territorial Gunners and then turning to the Home Guard and the Cadets. He indulges in occasional diversions from Hertfordshire's military history, and has written two small but important books on specialised aspects of British decorations for gallantry and contributes to the *Journal of the Orders and Medals Research Society*. After completing the Roll of Honour used for Special Operations Executive's F Section Memorial at Valençay in France, which was inaugurated in 1991, he edited a commemorative booklet published in both English and French. In recognition of his work in preserving and recording the history of military units raised in Hertfordshire, he was elected a Fellow of the Society of Antiquaries of London in 1991.